Modern Criminals

Trans-**action** Books

Modern Criminals

Edited by
JAMES F. SHORT, JR.

Trans-**action** Books

Published and distributed by
Aldine Publishing Company

The essays in this book originally appeared
in *Trans-action* Magazine

TA Book-8
Library of Congress Catalog Number: 70-96130

Contents

ACKNOWLEDGEMENTS

This volume is the product, first of all, of the authors, whose contributions to a fledgling journal have made it a medium of important substance. Equally important, it is a product of editorial leadership and operation, without which much of substance is ineffectively communicated and therefore ineffective in public dialogue and policy consideration. We are grateful for these contributions and hopeful that they will make a difference.

Preface

However diverse their attitudes and interpretations may sometimes be, social scientists are now entering a period of shared realization that the United States—both at home and abroad—has entered a crucial period of transition. Indeed, the much burdened word "crisis" has now become a commonplace among black militants, Wall Street lawyers, housewives, and even professional politicians.

For the past six years, *Trans*-action magazine has dedicated itself to the task of reporting the strains and conflicts within the American system. But the magazine has done more than this. It has pioneered in social programs for changing the society, offered the kind of analysis that has permanently restructured the terms of the "dialogue" between peoples and publics, and offered the sort of prognosis that makes for real alterations in social and political policies directly affecting our lives.

The work done in the pages of *Trans*-action has crossed

disciplinary boundaries. This represents much more than simple cross-disciplinary "team efforts." It embodies rather a recognition that the social world cannot be easily carved into neat academic disciplines. That, indeed, the study of the experience of blacks in American ghettos, or the manifold uses and abuses of agencies of law enforcement, or the sorts of overseas policies that lead to the celebration of some dictatorships and the condemnation of others, can best be examined from many viewpoints and from the vantage points of many disciplines.

This series of books clearly demonstrates the superiority of starting with real world problems and searching out practical solutions, over the zealous guardianship of professional boundaries. Indeed, it is precisely this approach that has elicited enthusiastic support from leading American social scientists for this new and dynamic series of books.

The demands upon scholarship and scientific judgment are particularly stringent, for no one has been untouched by the current situation. Each essay republished in these volumes bears the imprint of the author's attempt to communicate his own experience of the crisis. Yet, despite the sense of urgency these papers exhibit, the editors feel that many have withstood the test of time, and match in durable interest the best of available social science literature. This collection of *Trans*-action articles, then, attempts to address itself to immediate issues without violating the basic insights derived from the classical literature in the various fields of social science.

The subject matter of these books concerns social changes that have aroused the long-standing needs and present-day anxieties of us all. These changes are in organizational life styles, concepts of human ability and intelligence, changing patterns of norms and morals, the relationship of social conditions to physical and biological environments, and in the status of social science with national policy making.

This has been a decade of dissident minorities, massive shifts in norms of social conduct, population explosions and urban expansions, and vast realignments between nations of the world. The social scientists involved as editors and authors of this *Trans*-action series have gone beyond observation of these critical areas, and have entered into the vital and difficult tasks of explanation and interpretation. They have defined issues in a way making solutions possible. They have provided answers as well as asked the right questions. Thus, this series should be conceived as the first collection dedicated not to the highlighting of social problems alone, but to establishing guidelines for social solutions based on the social sciences.

THE EDITORS
Trans-action

On Criminals and Criminologists: An Introduction and Overview

James F. Short, Jr.

Academic disciplines are characterized—some would say "plagued"—by numerous conflicts, as for example between people of various methodological and theoretical persuasions, between specialists and generalists, and "pure" vs. "applied" scholars. Criminology has had more than its share of these and other types of internecine strife. Indeed, perhaps more than other special area of inquiry and practice, criminology has suffered from a sort of parochialism in all of these respects.

Public pressures to solve *the* crime problem and to protect society have led to inordinate public interest and political involvement in the phenomena with which we struggle. These phenomena are by definition a part of political processes and this very fact has led to endless debate among academics over the efficacy of such definitions in relation to the scientific study of human behavior, and to exasperation on the part of practitioners "wrestling with the beast" who desperately (albeit sometimes reluctantly) need help from their academic colleagues.

In part, one suspects, as a result of political and broad public interest in the phenomena of crime, sins of both omission and commission have occurred with respect to the focus of attention of criminology. Laws define who shall be considered criminal, though they leave much leeway in law enforcement processes—leeway subject to unequal degrees of control by persons located variously in the social structure. In the making of law, in their ability to secure protection under the law, and in advantages accruing from discretion in its enforcement, those with the greatest political and economic power benefit the most. Thus, the young and the economically and politically impotent have been the primary focus of attention not only of laws, but of criminologists. Laws are both more explicit and harsher concerning the behavior proscribed and the sanctions against property offenses that are committed by the poor (e.g., larceny, burglary, and robbery) than they are with respect to economic crimes of the "better classes" (e.g., embezzlement, fee-splitting, illegal financial manipulations, and large-scale tax evasion). Indeed, many types of law violation by persons of middle- and upper-class status are not defined as criminal at all, but rather as violations of civil and administrative law. Penalties in such cases less often involve incarceration and public stigma than do cases in violation of criminal law.

Until Edwin H. Sutherland forcefully called the academic community to task for its neglect of such matters in 1949, little heed was paid the phenomena he labelled *white collar* crime. Most criminologists were content to study prisoners, or at least officially adjudged criminals and delinquents, and they did not distinguish among different types of behavior for which such persons had been apprehended. Sutherland was also partly responsible, in 1939, for the increased attention paid *professional* crime, and his student and colleague Donald R. Cressey—represented in this volume by his paper on "The Respectable Criminal"—has made major contributions to our understanding of *organized* crime in this country.

Distinctions among these and other types of criminals has been paralleled by the development of a variety of typologies among juvenile delinquents. But there is much scholarly disagreement as to the value of such distinctions. On the one hand, several studies suggest the importance of distinguishing among different developmental patterns and behavioral "syndromes" among youngsters and adults who become embroiled with the law. Included are an impressive array of "subcultural" delinquents and offenders who are oriented variously with respect to violation of the law, some of whom specialize in particular types of offenses, such as check forgers, shoplifters, prostitutes, assaulters, murderers, rapists, homosexuals, drug addicts, and others. On the other hand, at the juvenile level in particular, studies focusing on delinquency in general have been able to account statistically for as much of the variance in the behavior of the youngsters studied as have "syndrome" explanations.

Something else "new" has been added to this debate. We have been reminded by a considerable body of research and theory that "crime" and "delinquency," "criminals" and "delinquents" are important social labels. Their application to particular types and episodes of behavior and to individuals and groups has important social consequences, both for the individuals so labelled and for the community. The degree to which the label is adopted by both parties influences the individual's conception of himself, his relations with peers and many others. It also provides a convenient definition for the community, which in modern urban society becomes especially important, as schools, places of employment, law enforcement officials and others must relate to and in many cases make decisions affecting large numbers of individuals. The labels "ex-con" and "delinquent" doubtless vary greatly in significance and attributed meaning. They are unlikely to be insignificant, however, and the experience of many years, as well as evidence from carefully controlled studies, suggests that they are often decidedly negative in their consequences.

We need to know a great deal more about these matters. Certainly with respect to adults, finer distinctions than those provided by the labels "criminal" and "noncriminal" appear to be necessary if we would understand and deal effectively with the multiplicity of behaviors so labelled. The very fact that adults have accumulated longer and more varied experience with occupational careers and relations with a variety of social institutions makes it unlikely that the development of patterns of behavior involving commission of crime will occur as a result of the operation of exactly the same forces and processes.

Similar variety is found in the behaviors labelled "delinquent." Yet, because of their position as the "younger generation," and relatively common institutional arrangements for their preparation for adult roles in society, "getting in trouble" for the young is more likely to involve common processes and consequences than is the case for their elders. However, many scholars have found it important to distinguish between various patterns of juvenile, as well as adult, involvement in law-violative behavior.

Both points of view are represented in this volume. We

begin with consideration of the young.

Probably no generation has been without its detractors. References to juvenile misbehavior have been found among the work of the most ancient scribes. Perhaps here it is the behavior of criminologists, rather than the youngsters, which is new. The first selection provides an apt example.

Robert J. Hamblin, Mark J. Abrahamson, and Robert L. Burgess consider a multiplicity of factors in relation to the delinquency of white and Negro teenagers in a low-income area in St. Louis. "Diagnosing" delinquency, as such, is their primary focus, and to this task they bring a variety of methods of data collection and measuring devices. Their findings will surprise many, and they illustrate well the behavioral effects, or correlates, of different social factors acting together within varying social and cultural contexts.

The next two papers concern a familiar context of delinquency, the juvenile gang, but their focus is very different.

Walter Miller seems to be telling us that nothing is really new under the sun concerning juvenile gangs and their behavior. One sex groups with peers on the corner or in the candy shop—it has always been thus. He reminds us that, despite widespread belief to the contrary, juvenile gangs still populate lower-class neighborhoods in many of our large cities, and they continue to be associated with serious law-violative behaviors. Miller relates such behavior among the groups he studied to the cultural traditions of the lower-class area in which they were located and to the dynamics of group leadership and relationships between different age groups in the community.

It is well to recall that Miller's study focuses attention on gang and lower-class life in a relatively stable community where such traditions have evolved over a considerable period of time. Not all lower-class communities are so characterized. Some have been torn by rapid and repeated transitions from óne ethnic group to another. The degree of stability and positive influence of traditional institutions and adult roles is also a variable characteristic among communities. In some respects, these matters vary along racial lines, as suggested in the article by Fred Strodtbeck and James Short.

"Why Gangs Fight" treats in some detail a few of the group mechanisms which produce delinquent behavior among gangs, and variations in such behavior related to subcultural differences. The context remains the lower-class adolescent gang, but the status mechanisms described appear to operate in a variety of other contexts as well.

Recent empirical and theoretical work concerning juvenile delinquency is extremely rich and varied. What is new in the behavior of young people, it appears, is related to Part III of the present volume, to be discussed shortly.

"Crimes, Victims, and the Police," by Phillip Ennis, reports findings from a study of the incidence of criminal victimization among a carefully selected sample of the U.S. population surveyed in 1965. The study was conducted for the President's Commission on Law Enforcement and Administration of Justice, better known as the Crime Commission. This survey reveals considerably higher rates of "ordinary" crimes committed against individuals than have been projected on the basis of the best national statistics. (It also suggests some of the reasons for attrition in the reporting of crime and in other steps involved in crime statistics.) Finally, Ennis touches on an extremely complex and important issue which has leapt into national prominence in recent years, namely, police power—or, more appropriately, "relocating the police in the political spectrum," a subject to which we will return in Part III.

Ennis' article reports a fresh approach to the problems of

measuring crime. The problem is crucial, not because it feeds the curiosity of academic researchers, but because inadequacies of measurement render difficult if not impossible realistic appraisal of the nature of crime and its causes, and the efficacy of attempts to cope with it. The Crime Commission concluded that "What is known about the trend of crime—in the total number of offenses; in the rates of offenses to population—and in the relationships of crime trends to change in the composition of the population—is almost wholly a product of statistics." By way of contrast, we note that much of the accumulated body of scientific knowledge and speculation concerning the nature and causes of crime is based on case studies of questionable representativeness, special statistical studies unrelated to official data sources, and theories related to variables for which official data are lacking or inadequate. Several imaginative attempts have been made in recent years to refine and elaborate data from official sources and to compare such data with information collected by other means. The need for more systematic and relevant data is great; for many types of research, statistics serve as the behavioral scientist's laboratory, allowing him to relate behavioral phenomena to characteristics of the population and to social conditions in a manner similar to the laboratory experiment of other scientists. There is need both for making present reporting systems more responsive to the data requirements of scientists, and for experimentation with new data systems such as the NORC survey described by Ennis.

The intricate and complicated relationships of a specific type of crime and its defining law, public attitudes and social and economic status, are well illustrated by the second article in this section, "Abortion Laws and Their Victims." This paper, by Alice Rossi, probes laws with respect to this controversial subject, their effects on the people concerned, and related public opinions.

Here the "criminals" are in fact victims, as has been suggested is the case in other types of behavior which neither directly nor indirectly harm the person or property of others, such as homosexuality and drug addiction. A distinction must be made between these behaviors and *related* acts which may and often do cause harm, as in the case of the person illegally performing an abortion or the victimization of another in support of a drug habit or in search of a homosexual partner. Alice Rossi shows that public opinion in the country is more permissive than the majority of laws relating to abortion, but that neither laws nor public opinion support the use of abortion as a birth-control technique—the chief reason women who seek abortions want them. Studies of the incidence and distribution of abortions suggest that abortion laws and much public opinion victimize the poor in particular. Well-educated women are more likely to find it possible to abort premarital pregnancies and their practice of contraceptive techniques after marriage is more reliable, while "poorly educated women who become pregnant, either have illegitimate children (particularly if they are Negro) or marry and have the first child within wedlock, and abort their later pregnancies." Alice Rossi examines the dilemmas of women who become pregnant and makes a strong plea for the right of "any women, whether married or not—to secure a safe abortion, upon her own request, at a reasonable fee, in a licensed hospital by a licensed and competent physician."

In the final selection in Part II, Donald R. Cressey is concerned with "respectable" people, not as victims of crime, but as criminals. While *opportunity* is an important aspect of the theory Cressey develops to explain such behavior, as it is in various attempts to explain other types of crime, Cressey stresses two other elements: (1) the belief that a personal financial problem is unshareable, and (2) most importantly, the individual's formulation of violation of financial trust in such a way as to define it as something other than criminal, thus protecting himself from this definition. Cressey cites evidence suggesting that verbalizations of the latter type, together with the influence and mutual support of associates (which is stressed in Sutherland's theory of differential association) may be an important factor in making possible the commitment of a variety of other types of crime by otherwise respectable people. Probably the most effective neutralization of law as an inhibitor of delinquent behavior is lack of belief in the law and in the efficacy of other regulatory agencies.

Crimes of a political nature are as old as the state, yet they have been very little studied by criminologists. Few recent texts in either criminology or juvenile delinquency even mention such criminals or the behavior that is classified in this manner. The four papers in Part III of this volume attempt to redress this situation.

Part III begins with research and commentary concerning assassination—political homicide. Carl Leiden's research paper, "Assassination in the Middle East," discusses a typology of motives for assassination with illustrations from that politically turbulent part of the world. He also discusses factors influencing the political impact of assassination. The second paper consists of thoughtful commentary following the assassination of Senator Robert F. Kennedy, by *Trans*-action Editor-in-Chief, Irving Louis Horowitz and Advisory Editor Herbert J. Gans.

Part III and the book conclude with two papers from researchers at the Disaster Research Center at Ohio State University. Russell Dynes and Enrico Quarantelli compare looting in natural disasters and in civil disturbances. From their own and other studies they find that looting is broadly participated in by local people and is very common in civil disturbances, but rare and with few participants, who are usually outsiders, in disasters; it is more selective in civil disorders, "focusing on particular types of goods or possessions, often symbolic of other values;" and in such instances it receives strong social support from some segments of the local community, while it is strongly and universally condemned in disaster situations. In both types of situations, they suggest, traditional individual property rights are redefined. In the face of disasters, a sort of community right of eminent domain takes precedence over individual rights, as the community seeks to save lives and avert further disaster. Private property is commonly appropriated, and is widely approved, for such purposes. But appropriation of property for private gain is condemned and often dealt with in the most severe way. The redefinition of property rights which occurs in civil disturbances, by way of contrast, involves conflict between local people on the one hand and, on the other, the law and the larger society. Dynes and Quarantelli remind us that the laws defining property rights are "based on *dominant conceptions* of property rights" (emphasis added). Civil disturbances, including looting, may be viewed as mass protests against these conceptions and, more basically, against the legitimacy of the social, economic and political system which fosters and protects them.

The second of these two articles, "Scapegoats, Villains, and Disasters," by Thomas E. Drabeck and Quarantelli, explores public reaction to disastrous occurrences in terms of assignment of responsibility to *individuals* vs. *the system*. They suggest that the former, which often takes the form of scapegoating, often obscures fundamental faults in the system and prevents their correction.

These varied papers suggest common themes of great importance related to crime and the political order. They are joined by a rising tide of politically relevant protests and confrontations, on college and university campuses, at political conventions, in the streets and parks and places of business of our cities. Such protests are not new in our history, as demonstrated by a recent report to the National Commission on the Causes and Prevention of Violence. On the basis of the most comprehensive historical and comparative study of violence ever undertaken, Hugh Davis Graham and Ted Robert Gurr, Task Force Co-Directors for the Commission, conclude that throughout American history and in much of the rest of the world, "One group's legitimate protest has been another group's illegal violence . . ."

"Legitimacy"—of the law and the systems it represents, as well as of protests and protestors—becomes a crucial question as we examine these political-criminal questions. Another Task Force of the Violence Commission reports that in the United States, unlike the Near East and many other parts of the world, assassination has rarely been utilized as a political tactic, either as part of the established "legitimate" system or in opposition to it. The Reconstruction period in the South, following the Civil War, provides one of the few examples of the use of assassination as a deliberate tactic in opposition to the prevailing system of government. This study also concludes that, with rare exceptions, assassination of public office-holders has not involved conspiracy. However, particularly since the massive expansion of executive power, beginning with Franklin D. Roosevelt and focusing on the presidency, that office has become particularly vulnerable. The conclusion of scholars who have studied the problem is that those who have made attempts on our Presidents' lives were demented individuals acting irrationally rather than on behalf of a carefully rationalized political strategy. It would be a great mistake, however, as Horowitz and Gans remind us, to take the absence of conspiracy as evidence that recent assassinations in this country are idiosyncratic and the result simply of personal pathology. If personal pathology is involved—and most assuredly it often is, as shown by the best evidence available—the evidence suggests also that it has been triggered by the climate of "fanaticism that is linked to reinforced nationalist claims or ethnic affiliations" and by an "American culture, which has condoned and even praised political violence while also condemning it." It is important, therefore, not to underestimate the structural and cultural forces involved in assassinations in this, as in other countries. For as the Violence Commission reports make clear, the climate of political violence in this country—in rhetoric and in action—stands today at a very high level, particularly compared with other modern western countries. Whether political violence is higher now than in the past is less important than the fact that public awareness of such violence surely is higher than ever before, except possibly during the Civil War. And this, together with our enormous wealth and technical capacity, gives hope for creative as opposed to panic solutions—for study *and* action, rather than study *instead of* action.

If the basic American political system has escaped major challenge to its legitimacy in the past, present events foreshadow such challenges. This is the essence of what is new in crime and delinquency, and it gives a sense of great urgency to the search for solutions. For the protests of blacks and college students, whether against second-class citizenship, foreign policy and a war of which the majority of U. S. citizens disapproves, or based on issues of a more local institutional character, are to a large and perhaps increasing extent political in nature. The system is being challenged by the more militant, and much larger numbers are sympathetic with many of their specific protests. Even the "silent majority" of blacks and students and the "forgotten Americans," though they may support the system and even cling to halcyon memories of bygone days, seem willing to challenge its fundamental tenets, whether in the name of "law and order" or in the name of some aspect of the system which they choose to assign primacy, such as "free, private enterprise," "participatory democracy," "freedom," or "property."

An element of great importance in this picture is the politicization of the police—not only in behalf of their own job conditions and benefits, but in terms of some of the fundamentally political and moral issues that are the source of conflict and the basis for activities in the course of which people frequently become involved in behavior defined and treated as criminal. The fact that the police are charged with the responsibility of maintaining law and order often involves them in enforcing political decisions not legally required and in fact at times in violation of basic constitutional guarantees. The fact that the police sometimes take stands against legal protest, and act illegally in its suppression, adds fuel to the flame of charges and evidence concerning police "brutality." In this way the legitimacy of the system receives yet another challenge.

Finally, it should be clear that no theory based on personal pathology, or on the responsibility of "riff-raff" for violent aspects of contemporary protest and confrontation is empirically defensible. While it is true that some juvenile gangs appear to be developing considerable interest and sophistication in complex economic and political matters, the evidence is overwhelming that participation in urban riots is widespread among educational and occupational groups in the ghetto, and that antiwar and student protest receive their major impetus from middle-class elements of the society, especially students from middle-class backgrounds and their teachers, from the clergy and from many persons in other professions and in business.

And so we come full circle. "Ordinary" crime, gang delinquency, and crime by "respectables" are facilitated by belief systems and associations which negate or neutralize the legitimacy and therefore the effectiveness of regulating systems. A major task with respect to all these types of criminal behavior, as well as crime which results from more specifically political beliefs and activities, thus has to do with the legitimacy of systems of control. A major consideration in this respect is the justice of these systems —or, more specifically, the *perceived* justice of these systems. And so justice must be added to law and order. Again, this is primarily a collective matter. For, while individual justice is important to the individual, social and political movements relate to the experiences and grievances of groups, and political systems, laws and enforcement procedures are the product of group efforts. Solutions to problems related to crime, therefore, are likely to require group efforts and programs if they are to be successful.

At the individual level, one's "stake in conformity" has been found to be related to juvenile delinquency. That is, those youngsters who develop a stake—financial, reputational, emotional, etc.—in conforming to the norms of society and its institutions do not ordinarily become involved in behavior considered criminal or otherwise deviant. The application of this notion to other types of crime, as well as to the beliefs and activities of those who protest, is most suggestive. The relation between the perceived legitimacy of institutions and one's stake in conformity to their expectations would seem to be clear and straightforward. It may be neither, but the evidence points in this direction and it is a good hypothesis to test—in theory and in action.

Debate concerning the nature of crime and delinquency —their causes and cures—is lively and continuing, as certainly it should be. While scholars are likely to emphasize their differences, however, there is also much evidence of agreement. This, too, is as it should be. For, no matter how differentiated the behavior under study—among "deviants" as well as among those who define and react to them—the actors are human and the subject matter of concern is human behavior.

The study of such behavior at last shows signs of becoming a part of the "mainstream" of behavioral science inquiry and application. A mark of this, perhaps, is the fact that only two of the ten articles here reprinted are authored (or coauthored) by scholars whose primary identity is that of criminologist, or student of deviant behavior, including crime and delinquency. Even these, and all of the others, have other identities—as do most criminologists nowadays: as social psychologists, methodologists, theorists, or students of urban society, social organization, occupations, socialization, small groups, political science or political sociology, literature and the arts, etc.

We have argued that, to an increasing extent, behavior considered criminal—and societal reaction to that behavior —are by various means becoming politicized. The problems of those who protest, whether for general or specific cause (for example, ghetto residents vs. the victims of abortion laws or citizens outraged as a result of disaster), are increasingly viewed and acted upon as political matters. The reactions of "respectable" citizens to victimization or its perceived threat are freighted with problems related to their experience with and confidence in political elements of social control, chiefly the police. Even some juvenile gangs have abandoned their customarily apolitical character. Black militancy finds a cutting edge among black high school students, and white backlash similarly finds major strength among the young.

How politicization will influence the more traditional delinquent behavior among adolescents, and the behavior of those who protest, by demonstration or riot, and how it will alter the perception of such behavior and such people by members of the larger society, and relations with them, are matters that remain to be determined. That it will have important consequences for all concerned can hardly be doubted.

Many issues and many points of view are discussed in these pages. Debate concerning issues such as these is healthy; indeed, it is essential. Implications for social action are rarely clear and never specific. They should be carefully explored and formulated, tried and tested; our knowledge and ability to cope with significant social problems will thereby be greatly increased, and our confidence and strength as a society much advanced.

Washington State University   *James F. Short, Jr.*
Pullman, Washington

FURTHER READING SUGGESTED BY THE EDITOR

Becker, Howard S., *Outsiders,* New York: The Free Press, 1963.

Campbell, Angus and Schuman, Howard, "Racial Attitudes in Fifteen American Cities," *Supplemental Studies for the National Advisory Commission on Civil Disorders,* USGPO, 1968.

Clinard, Marshall B. and Quinney, Richard, *Criminal Behavior Systems: A Typology,* New York: Holt, Rinehart and Winston, Inc., 1967.

Cloward, Richard A. and Ohlin, Lloyd E., *Delinquency and Opportunity,* New York: The Free Press, 1960.

Cohen, Albert K., *Delinquent Boys,* Glencoe, Ill.: The Free Press, 1954.

Cressey, Donald C., *Theft of a Nation*, New York: Harper and Row, 1969.

Gibbons, Don C., *Society, Crime and Criminal Careers*, New York: Prentice-Hall, 1968.

Hirschi, Travis, *Causes of Delinquency*, Berkeley: University of California Press, 1969.

Matza, David, *Becoming Deviant*, New York: Prentice-Hall, 1969.

National Advisory Commission on Civil Disorders:, *Report*, USGPO, 1968.

National Commission on the Causes and Prevention of Violence: Task Force Reports.

    Campbell, James S., Stang, David and Sahid, Joseph R., *Report of the Task Force on Law and Law Enforcement*, USGPO, 1969.

    Graham, Hugh Davis and Gurr, Ted Robert, *Violence in America: Historical and Comparative Studies*, Volumes 1 and 2, USGPO, 1969.

    Kirkham, James, Levy, Sheldon and Crotty, William, *Report of the Task Force on Assassinations and Political Violence*, USGPO, 1969.

    Mulvihill, Donald and Tumin, Melvin, *Crimes of Violence*, USGPO, 1969.

    Newton, George and Zimring, Franklin E., *Firearms and Violence in American Life*, USGPO, 1969.

    Skolnick, Jerome H., *The Politics of Protest: Violent Aspects of Protest and Confrontations*, USGPO, 1969.

Platt, Anthony M., *The Child Savers*, Chicago: University of Chicago Press, 1969.

President's Commission on Law Enforcement and Administration of Justice, *The Challenge of Crime in a Free Society*, USGPO, 1967; *Task Force Report: Juvenile Delinquency and Youth Crime*, USGPO, 1967.

Rossi, Peter H., Berk, Richard A.; Boesel, David P.; Eidson, Bettye K. and Groves, W. Eugene; "Between White and Black: The Faces of American Institutions in the Ghetto," *Supplemental Studies for the National Advisory Commission on Civil Disorders*, USGPO, 1968.

Schur, Edwin M., *Crimes Without Victims*, Englewood Cliffs, N.J.: Prentice-Hall, 1965.

Sellin, Thorsten and Wolfgang, Marvin E., *The Measurement of Delinquency*, New York: Wiley, 1964.

Short, James F., Jr., and Strodtbeck, Fred L., *Group Process and Gang Delinquency*, Chicago: University of Chicago Press, 1965.

Sutherland, Edwin H., *The Professional Thief*, Chicago, University of Chicago Press, 1937; *White Collar Crime*, New York: Dryden, 1949.

Wheeler, Stanton, ed., *Controlling Delinquents,* New York: Wiley, 1968.

Wolfgang, Marvin E. and Ferracuti, Franco, *The Subculture of Violence: Towards an Integrated Theory in Criminology,* London: Tavistock Publication, 1967.

Diagnosing Delinquency

ROBERT L. HAMBLIN/MARK J. ABRAHAMSON
ROBERT L. BURGESS

Juvenile delinquents have been called many things, not only by parents, the public, and police, but by social scientists as well. Delinquency has been blamed on immoral behavior, inherited defects of character, mental deficiency, mental disorder ("a psychiatric symptom that happens to be against the law"), or lack of conscience or control. It has also been described as a "normal response to abnormal conditions"—presumably what any red-blooded young person would do to acquire respectable satisfactions if cut off by poverty or racial discrimination from respectable methods of achievement.

To the social scientist, there are two aspects to juvenile delinquency: there must be some behavior by an adolescent; and just as important, the adult community must become aware of that behavior and condemn it.

Legally, a delinquent act committed by an adolescent is one which, if performed by an adult and detected would result after trial and conviction in punishment, probably including prison.

But such a narrow definition raises many more questions than it begins to answer. Delinquency does not exist in isolation. The concept did not spring fully formed, from the brow of an overwrought sociologist. Behind each delinquent are social, psychological, and environmental seeds planted in the past; ahead of him are fruits still to come, probably socially unpleasant; the soil around his roots has many nutrients in common with those that nourish us all —and some which do not.

What causes juvenile delinquency? Or, at least, how may we predict delinquent behavior? Specifically, what are the links between behavior we call delinquent and the actual problems in education, racial discrimination, work, sex, and growing up that individual delinquents have?

How does delinquency differ between whites and Negroes? Between boy and girls? What *instigators* seem to push youths toward delinquency? What *inhibitors* hold them back?

The authors of this article sought to find some answers to these questions. No attempt was made to formulate new theories; in fact, hypotheses were derived specifically and deliberately from major current research and ideas. Since we were searching for methods of prediction, we did not, at this stage, draw sharp distinctions between symptom and cause—the chills and fever that lead to successful diagnosis are often as useful to a physician as the actual bacteria he may some day hope to isolate.

Data were collected by routine methods. In treating that data, new measuring devices were developed from recent research in the rising field of psychophysics, which allowed intensive and accurate mathematical and statistical analysis. We also used and demonstrated a concept which, though by no means new, is still not often understood by the general public: the concept of *interaction*. With living creatures a whole is almost always much more than the sum of its parts. Botanists a half century ago found that if they watered certain plants, they might increase growth about 20 percent, and if they fertilized them, growth might increase perhaps 10 percent; but if they did both together, the growth might suddenly jump as high as 200 percent. The combination interacted, bringing about what amounted to a kind of metabolic explosion. A youth may be mildly instigated toward delinquency by failure in school, or he may lack inhibitions as a result of poor home training, with no obvious effect on behavior. But if both occur together, the results are likely to be dramatic, and he might well become a police case.

We investigated and studied white and Negro boys and girls, age thirteen through nineteen, living around the central business district of St. Louis, a low-income, high-crime area. We also interviewed their mothers and studied the relationships between children and parents.

We started with one main assumption: that delinquency is an effort to cope with a difficult environment which severely limits the opportunities of an adolescent to acquire legitimately the things held dear by his group. What the delinquent wants is fundamentally not much different from what we all want; but he finds our routine and respectable methods of fulfillment pretty well closed to him. Delinquency is indeed a "normal reaction to abnormal conditions": it can give the delinquent money and possessions; it can give him status and prestige—not only among his friends, who are perhaps most important to him, but in the larger community as well.

Delinquency can do more; it can reduce psychological tensions. Adolescents approaching adulthood are subject to great pressures. These are especially acute among the underprivileged, who have few of the compensations that money or status can buy. But delinquency can reduce these tensions and relieve pressure; many youths will turn to it as naturally as they would swallow medicine to relieve pain.

What then are the factors that, in combination, instigate delinquency? They fall under three general headings:

(1) difficulties in coping successfully with problems of education;

(2) difficulties in work;

(3) difficulties in growing up to be a man or a woman —that is, in assuming the appropriate sex roles.

Whether these troubles had already been experienced, were anticipated, or were feared was not basic: they led to delinquency in all four of the groups studied.

The relative importance of these instigators, however, varies with sex and race. For example, delinquency among the boys, both white and Negro, was highly impulsive— not inhibited much by fear of punishment—whether prison, hellfire, or merely getting caught. Obviously then this is one reason why the conventional "get tough" philosophy of correction, based heavily on instilling fear of punishment, has not worked well with delinquent boys—who make up the vast majority of offenders. It might, however, the study showed, have a much greater effect on girls, who *are* strongly inhibited by fear of discovery and punishment.

Shoplifting turned out to be by far the best indicator of delinquency. At first this may seem surprising; to many people shoplifting appears trivial, more a prank than a crime, even a phase through which many adolescents pass. But it takes on more serious aspects among the poor, who may use it to supplement the family income. It is a crime well understood by women, often encouraged by mothers, who set the example, and who frequently dominate slum families. Those young people who shoplifted were also those most likely to go in for more serious delinquency.

Since shoplifting is both a juvenile crime and the prime indicator of other juvenile crimes, it was used throughout the detailed study that follows as the definition of delinquency itself. Except possibly in a legal sense, "delinquency" is not one phenomenon but a great number, not all related. And no one thing causes or predicts *delinquency* as a whole, any more than a single kind of bacteria or a single symptom causes or predicts *disease.*

The factors found by the study to be related to delinquency are listed in order of increasing importance. Sexual difficulties and conflicts, found to be major causes of delinquency, are considered last.

Conflict between a teenager and his parents about the value of school will often encourage delinquency.

This is particularly predictable among those Negro boys who like and value school, and feel they can succeed, when they encounter the opposition of parents—especially mothers—who believe they should be out earning money.

Such a parental attitude may seem incomprehensible to middle-class parents; but it is common among the poor. Some poor parents, of course, recognize what education may mean for the future of their children and will make great sacrifices to keep them in school. But many Negroes, unskilled, uneducated, and often unemployeed, know few educated people who could serve as good examples; the value of education for the future seems like so much deceitful pie in the sky, compared to the realities of the present. Even if the boy's pay should come to so little that he could contribute almost nothing, he would be able to support himself and be less of a drain on the family.

Caught between such an attitude and his own desire to continue school, boxed in by the further knowledge that discrimination and lack of funds will limit his education and future, the Negro youth becomes ripe for delinquency if one or more other interacting elements is present.

It should be noted that the Negro boys described here are often among the most promising—ambitious, intelligent and able. Except for parental opposition, their chances for education and success would probably be good. In the first issue of *Trans*-action S. M. Miller pointed out that the "high-aspiring" school dropout is very different from the "low aspirer." The "high aspirer" has great potentialities for good if he could be kept in school. When these high-aspiring Negro boys quit and turn delinquent, the community suffers a double loss. It loses their potential talents and abilities, and it also suffers the many different costs of delinquency—police, prisons, stolen goods, and terror.

With delinquent *white boys,* it is more often educational than parental frustration that pushes them toward trouble. They know the value of education; but they do not have, or do not believe they have, the ability or chance to succeed. Desire and discouragement interact: the more the boy wants to succeed, coupled with pessimism about succeeding, the greater the frustration and the stronger the temptation to relieve his tensions by law-breaking.

The most predictable school pattern for delinquent Negro girls is almost exactly opposite that for Negro boys. The greater their personal school failures and the greater the scholastic success of their parents, the more likely they are to come to trouble. Again the interaction: a single element—simple failure on the girl's part, for instance—is not enough; both must be present.

With white girls too, the combination of school factors associated with delinquency differs from the other groups. Low grades and truancy, confronted by parental pressure to succeed, creates the interaction that most encourages delinquency among white girls.

The Negro boy who finds a job is less likely to be delinquent than the one who does not. A Negro boy will often believe that his inability to find work—or to keep it if he does find it—is the fault of a society that discriminates, not his personal failure. The cards are stacked against him. But when he finds and holds a job he becomes confident that he can fit into the society and take care of himself—that he can beat the game, stacked deck and all.

Interestingly, a Negro boy's adjustment and confidence will often grow with the *number* of jobs he has had— something which might, in another context, indicate uncertainty and instability. The Negro boy feels, however, that if he has already had several jobs, he can get another when he needs it. A boy who has had only one job, however good, cannot be quite so sure.

A job will often make the difference between trouble and adjustment for a white boy too. However, his greatest push toward delinquency occurs when there is a strong conflict between his mother's pressures on him to get a "good" high-status job and his resistance. Sometimes he believes he cannot get such a job and that his mother does not understand his problems. But he may actually prefer a lower-level job—working with his hands rather than in an office—or he may want to continue his education. The more intense the conflict, the greater the chance of delinquency.

With white boys, too, there is an apparently contradictory sidelight: the more one wants a part-time job—usually considered a mark of stability—the more he is apt to turn delinquent. However, closer analysis shows that few white boys who were questioned thought they actually had any chance for such jobs, so the common pattern of frustration is once more present: the conflict between what they want and what they feel they must accept.

In their job-seeking, Negro girls face this same conflict in aggravated form. They want good jobs; they can't get them. Their mothers often come to embody and personify the voices of harsh reality, the death of hopes and dreams. Negro girls cannot pick and choose; they must take the jobs they can get—usually hard dirty work, at poor pay—and consider themselves lucky to have any at all; the glossy white careers described in the slick magazines are not for people like them.

The greater the conflict between dream and reality, between their job desires and their mothers', the greater the temptation to blow the lid off their frustrations and turn delinquent. Like the Negro boys, they have the dubious solace of being able to blame their failures, with considerable justice, on discrimination rather than on themselves. But this usually tends to increase frustration, and to relieve them of feeling much personal responsibility for their plight—or for their subsequent actions.

Sexual conflicts play a very strong part in motivating delinquency—and a very complex one. In this drama the mother-child relationship is the focal point.

As a Negro mother exerts increasing pressure on her son to avoid becoming delinquent—and as she worries more and more about his being caught—the likelihood rises rapidly that what she fears most will come true. If he dislikes her—and if she attempts to supervise him closely —the condition is aggravated. This is not a new finding, nor confined to delinquents—evidence from many studies shows that close, tough supervision generally creates enmity and tension.

Should the Negro boy, however, like his mother, and if her control is loose, exerted mostly through other children, then the pressure toward delinquency will lessen.

Slum families are frequently female-dominated. Often the father is dead or has fled, or the children are illegitimate. Where the father does live with the family, he may seem to be a failure as a breadwinner, or they would not be in such sorry plight; so the mother sometimes must, and often does, take over the dominant role. Her values, attitudes, and actions must, to a large extent therefore, mold her children, and drastically affect their lives.

This female domination causes deep disturbances in the sexuality and sexual identification of her sons, and forms one of the major roots for white male delinquency. If the white boy is overly attached to his mother, whether he realizes it or not, the way he thinks about himself as he grows to manhood will become confused and hesitant. His ties to mother can hold him back from marriage—even from sexual relations with girls. Often, when he does marry, he prefers to stay at home and let his wife earn the living. Since unskilled jobs are more plentiful for women than for men, this may be an increasing trend.

Specifically then, the push to delinquency increases among white boys to the extent that their mothers' influence governs them, and to the extent that their identities as developing men are confused. When a mother encourages shoplifting, her son will generally follow. If she rejects him for any reason, these pressures will interact—the desire to do anything to please her, even shoplifting, will become very great.

The potentially delinquent white boy who follows the above pattern is most often a loner, with few friends of either sex. He will, nevertheless, form the habit of going frequently to social agencies—and from one to the other. At first glance, this appears a healthy practice—after all, don't real delinquents hang around street corners with birds of like feather rather than around respectable community centers?

But this restless movement from agency to agency is a form of desperate search, not only for friends but for identity—a measure of loneliness and dependence. It is a ~~symptom~~, and a predictor, of the maladjustment that drives many white boys into reformatories.

With Negro girls, the sexual frustrations and conflicts that push them to delinquency are both more simple and more complex.

First, the pressures on them tend to leave them uncertain how to handle sex itself. Heavy and intimate petting is the accepted practice. Their feelings and affections, and the persistence of their boy friends, push them on toward sexual consummation—to resist must bring strong frustration and conflict. But to go on merely means exchanging one set of tensions and problems for what are perhaps worse ones. They fear pregnancy, trouble with parents, the criticisms and loss of friends. The two opposite trends collide and form an interaction: the stronger the desire for intercourse, and the stronger they are urged, or try, to hold back, the more likely that they will relieve their tensions by delinquency.

Delinquent Negro girls, like the other groups, suffer from confused sex identity and the tensions and insecurity it causes. As their liking for father increases, so does shoplifting; as the dislike for girls in school and neighborhood increases, so does delinquency. Finally, those Negro girls who could get married easily if they wanted to, but don't want to, are the most delinquent. To grow up and to accept the responsibilities of adulthood is difficult for any adolescent; it is almost impossible for those who have not really learned what sex they are, or how to accept it.

The white girl delinquents were most easily predicted.

They are also perhaps the most interesting of all cases studied.

As mentioned, the female-dominated household is very prominent in slum neighborhoods, and its standards tend to be handed down from generation to generation. The white girl delinquent is her mother's loving daughter.

Mama works and supports the family—so probably will daughter when and if she marries. Mother dosen't like men, especially *that* man, the father—and neither does daughter. Mother, although aggressively antimasculine, nevertheless assumes the male role of head of the house and so has a confused sex identification—so does daughter, who seldom likes the girls she knows.

Partially to support the family, mother engages in stealing and shoplifting, often encouraging her children; mother knows best, and daughter follows her example. Men are no good—mother's husband, especially—and illicit sex allows a woman more freedom and control than marriage, so daughter tends to want children out of wedlock— often even in preference to marriage. Good daughters, in short, get into trouble with the law; bad daughters settle down, get married, and conform.

The delinquent white girl, of course, is subject to counter-pressures from other boys and girls and the community. Often her troubles can be avoided if, before the delinquent pattern is established, friends pressure her into marriage or at least into a satisfactory sex relationship. Where petting steadily stops short of intercourse—a sure sign of internal conflict, and usually of rejection of boys—the chance for delinquency goes up. Where intercourse occurs and continues, instigation toward delinquency is reduced: first, apparently, because the white girl has decided that she is a woman after all, and being one isn't so bad; and second, because she often establishes a satisfactory relationship with that strange creature, a boy.

Interestingly, the tendency toward delinquency is less if mother is a messy housekeeper. The dirtier mother's household, the cleaner is apt to be daughter's police record. Here cleanliness is not next to godliness, but to lawlessness. Mother's messiness may push the daughter away from identifying with her and with her views of life.

From society's viewpoint, delinquency is the loss of a battle between internal forces that impel youths toward lawbreaking, and inhibitors that might slow them down. Delinquency results when massive pressures accumulate against weakened self-control and societal control.

As noted, delinquent boys are little restrained by fear of being found out and punished. Their acts are impulsive—or compulsive. They want their rewards now, and their crimes are often poorly planned, bizarre, and made up on the spur of the movement. The instigators do not have to be very strong, since the interacting inhibitors are weak.

Girls weigh their chances of getting caught and being punished much more deliberately and rationally than do boys; fear is a strong deterrent. If the chances of detection are minor, therefore, they are more strongly instigated toward delinquency. However, generally, since their inhibitors are stronger than those of boys, the pressures that make them break the law must also be stronger.

A realistic program of controlling delinquency must consider this difference between the sexes. Threats and punishment may well stop a girl. They are not as likely to stop a boy; they may actually motivate him to more antisocial acts. Also, such a program must not consider the problems these individuals face as though they exist in isolation and can be treated separately—as agency-confined welfare planners sometimes treat them. Educational and job difficulties, sex, race, growing up, and self-realization—all these work and compound together to make delinquency; and they reach a different balance and intensity in each adolescent.

The picture of delinquents that emerges from this study is one of confused and harassed young people, swept and tormented by contending tensions and problems. The mathematical analysis of behavior is often accused of ignoring the human in favor of the computation—of dealing, in effect, with mathematically created automatons rather than flesh and blood. But this is certainly not true here.

What could be more human, for example, than the young Negro girl pitting her frail hopes of a good job against her mother's stern admonition to face the hard facts? What more human than the white boy going from one social agency to another, seeking on every bulletin board, on every announcement of a dance or ping-pong tournament, some hint of his own identity, some indication that he belongs somewhere?

March 1964

Why Gangs Fight

JAMES F. SHORT, JR./FRED STRODTBECK

*Big Jake, leader of the Potentates, had been "cooling it"
over the fall and winter. However, Guy, leader of the Vice
Kings, with whom the Potentates were often at war,
warned: "Better watch Big Jake—he has to do something."
Why? "He's got to build that rep again. He's been gone
—now he's got to show everybody he's back!"*

> —report from a director of detached
> workers with juvenile gangs

Like Big Jake, Duke, of the King Rattlers, had also been
in jail. Before his internment he had been known for his
self-possession—for being a "cool" leader. Although a
capable and active fighter when he thought it necessary,
he never lost his head and was very effective in negotiation,
conciliation, and control. When he came out of jail his
leadership and his personal future were threatened and
uncertain, and he became belligerent, aggressive, and apparently reckless—with the approval of his gang. Once

33

things settled down for him, however, he reverted to the cool behavior that had made him such an effective leader.

As with leaders of nations, the qualities that raise boys to the tops of juvenile gangs are not necessarily those that best qualify them to stay there, or to rule. "A good suitor may not make a good husband, or a good campaigner a good president." Moreover gangs, though they may admire the fighting campaigner, are often more difficult to control than nations; members who feel abused can sometimes simply drop out, as citizens cannot.

These restrictions, however, do not limit fighting between gangs. Here a leader can work off his aggressions, show off his fighting prowess, and win prestige and popularity with his gang, making his position more secure. As with nations, tyrannizing outsiders is always more acceptable. A despot is someone who abuses his own people; if he attacks and tyrannizes other groups, he is a great and victorious leader, leading enthusiastic followers on to glory.

Juvenile gang leaders invest a great deal in their fighting reputations. Leadership and delinquency must therefore go together. In nearly all gangs we studied, over a three year period, we found that skill in fighting was highly valued, whether or not the gang itself had a fighting "rep." A fight often occurred because a gang, or its leaders, simply could not tolerate a real or implied threat to whatever reputation they had.

Some gangs are definitely "conflict oriented." Fighting is a major and necessary activity for them and a means of acquiring respect, admiration, and prestige within them. They must and do fight often. They have a heavy investment in—and therefore motivation toward—combat. Their leadership, reputation, and status are under constant challenge—anytime they falter some other gang will try to make them fall. They must be prepared for defense—indeed, they believe they must attack from time to time before others attack them, and to remind possible enemies to beware. "We are the mighty Vice Kings!" a leader will shout in challenge—much as Beowulf, using other names, might have done. The very titles and roles they create for themselves reflect the warlike stance—"war counselor," "armorer." These offices need not be clearly or formally defined or even performed; but they are recognized and given deference, and competition for them is fierce.

"Conflict" of course need not always involve major war —the primary purpose of battle is to prove oneself, not to capture anything. The kind of guerrilla combat such gangs engage in was well illustrated in the following abstract of a detached worker's incident report:

"I was sitting talking to the Knights, re-emphasizing my stand on guns, because they told me they had collected quite a few and were waiting for the Vice Kings to start trouble. I told them flatly that it was better that I got the gun than the police. They repeated that they were tired of running from the Vice Kings and that if they gave them trouble they were fighting back.

"I looked out of the car and noticed two Vice Kings and two girls walking down the street. William then turned around and made the observation that there were about fifteen or twenty Vice Kings across the street in the alley, wandering up the street in ones or twos.

"The Vice Kings encountered Commando (the leader) Jones, and a couple of other Knights coming around the corner. The Vice Kings yelled across to Commando and his boys, and Commando yelled back. I got out to cool Commando down, since he was halfway across the street daring them to do something. I grabbed him and began to pull him back.

"But the Vice Kings were in a rage, and three came across the street yelling that they were mighty Vice Kings. At this point, along came Henry Brown with a revolver, shooting. Everybody ducked and the Vice Kings ran. I began to throw Knights into my car because I knew that the area was 'hot.'

"In the car the boys were extremely elated. 'Baby, did you see the way I swung on that kid?' 'Man, did we tell them off?' 'Did you see them take off when I leveled my gun?' 'You were great, baby . . .'

"The tension was relieved. They had performed well and could be proud . . ."

No doubt the Vice Kings too felt the thrill of having faced conflict and come off well. They had met great danger bravely, and had a good alibi for not having won unquestioned victory—the enemy had a gun. The Knights, on their part also had an alibi—the worker had intervened. Both sides therefore won, and could mutually share satisfaction and enhanced reputation. Gang combat is not necessarily a winner-take-all game. No one need be defeated. The two gangs had "played the game" according to the standards of their "community"; they had been rewarded, and law and order were now restored. The larger society too profits from a no-loser game. Of course, results are not always so harmless. Boys and gangs are often beaten and people and property often injured in this "game."

Threats to the status of a leader can result in violence to whole gangs; but the process is more complicated than it seems. Threat to leadership is merely a special case of "status management," which involves all gang boys. How can high status best be achieved and maintained in the continuing and risky give-and-take of gang life?

Several kinds of threats to status are covered by the broad conception of status management. They are well illustrated in the elements involved in a "humbug"—a general brawl—that our workers witnessed and recorded.

Jim, the detached worker, had taken his gang, the North Side Vice Kings, to a professional basketball game at the Chicago Amphitheater. The boys were in good spirits, but restless and volatile. Duke, the strongest leader, had been drinking. He sat near a younger group, the Junior Chiefs. He was friendly to them but obnoxious to venders and others, and was generally putting on a show for the younger boys.

Duke announced that he was going to buy some beer— he had recently turned twenty-one. The worker told him that beer was out when they were on an officially sponsored activity. Duke bought it anyway, and after an argument in which Duke kept mentioning his age, Jim took the beer from him. Duke became abusive to the worker and other spectators; and the other Vice Kings also acted up. Jim then announced that the entire group had to leave immediately.

On the way out they met another group, the South Side Rattlers. As they passed, Duke "fatmouthed" one of them and blows were exchanged. The Rattlers, at first confused, retaliated and the humbug was on, while their workers, caught off guard, tried vainly to separate them.

A third group, the Cherokees, now happened on the scene. Having a grudge against the Vice Kings, they waited for no further invitation. "No one stopped to get an explanation of what was going on. The fellows just looked up, saw the fighting, and joined in." The Rattlers, apparently frightened by a couple of knives and a pistol, had started to run, and the fighting might have died had the

Cherokees stayed out.

The police partially broke up the battle, but a new round of insults started it again. A fourth group, the Midget Vice Kings arrived; hearing challenge and counter-challenge, they too gave battle, siding with the Vice Kings.

After the combat, the detached workers reported that all three major groups involved talked about going home to get their "stuff" (weapons) and preparing to fight. The Rattlers, having been forced to retreat, were especially disturbed and made many threats. However, when the police came up and escorted them to their car, eliminating all possibility of further humbugs, they acted relieved and happy. On the way home they teased each other about running.

One group—the Junior Chiefs—had not been challenged, or otherwise received any "status threats." Not very surprisingly, they did not fight, and stayed and watched the basketball game.

The other gangs, however, did feel their reputations and "manhood" threatened. Elements of threat included:

The worker publicly ignored and downgraded Duke's newly achieved adulthood.

Following this, he degraded him in the eyes of his special, younger, audience, the Junior Chiefs—and of his own gang, of which he was supposed to be a leader.

He publicly humiliated and degraded all the rest of the Vice Kings by ordering them to leave, like a bunch of kids who could not be trusted to behave in public. This too he did before the Junior Chiefs—an act which immediately downgraded them in the gang world—and before adults, who could immediately identify them as "kids."

Searching for an outlet for rage and frustration, and for a means to rebuild their shattered "reps," the Vice Kings encountered the Rattlers. They attacked them. Now

the reputations of the Rattlers (and later of the Cherokees) were threatened, and *they* counter retaliated.

Yet, for all the ferocity, the fights were shortlived.
Every group except the Vice Kings, who had been most
threatened, were brought under control fairly quickly and
stayed to see the basketball game—only the Vice Kings
missed it. Moreover, despite talk of retaliation, the humbug was self-contained; in the following months there was
no more humbugging between these groups. The fight
served the usual purpose of upholding reputations and
preserving the images of street warriors ready for combat.

Closer analysis, however, reveals more to the story. What
happened to the ferocious-warrior image after the fights
were stopped? And why so easily stopped? Also, not all
the boys fought. Except for the Vice Kings, each group
contained some boys who stayed out. Careful review suggests that those most deeply involved in the fighting were
the core gang-members—the leaders and those who wanted
to be leaders. Not all gang members—and not all gangs—
have the same investment in rep and status. Certainly no
gang rules or standards, spoken or implied, require that
all boys fight every time, even under these provocative
circumstances.

Gang rules and expectations do influence the behavior
of members; but that influence is not clear cut, and depends mostly on the situation. Gangs are fluid; members
change; boys come and go for days or weeks at a time,
and unless they are leaders, or important core members,
they are hardly missed. Under such circumstances, the
group leaders cannot make members—especially fringe
members—conform or give obedience by threatening ex-
pulsion or withdrawal of privileges. Most of the gang
leaders we studied were surprisingly conciliatory within
the group. But they had a special interest in making mem-

bers want to belong to a gang with a good reputation.

This article is concerned primarily with juvenile gangs whose status is built around conflict. But it must be emphasized that, despite prevalent stereotypes, juvenile gangs are not all conflict oriented, and value systems may vary among them as among other human groupings. A "retreatist" gang, which built its value system around the effect of dope, provides a dramatic contrast.

Although criticized and ridiculed repeatedly by other gangs for their cowardice and lack of manhood, the retreatists seldom responded to taunts, and always retreated from combat. They did not worry about their reputations as fighters—they had none—and did not think them important—in fact, they thought the conflict oriented gangs to be "square." Directly challenged to join other white gangs in repelling Negro "wade-in" demonstrators on a beach in Chicago, they got "high" on pills and unconcernedly played cards during the entire incident.

The basis of camaraderie—what was important—to the drug users was "kicks." Past and present exploits—their legends of valor—continually recounted, concerned "high" experiences and "crazy" behavior rather than bravery or toughness. "You get the feeling," a member of the team of research observers said, "that whatever the activity of the moment, the guys will talk about it in relation to dope —how taking dope affects their participation in the activity."

Even their humor revolved around the effect of dope— the antics of friends under the influence. They laughed about the boy who kept trying to start a junked car that had no motor. Another one, beaten by a Chinese laundryman he tried to rob, "was so doped out of his mind" that he asked the arriving police to arrest the other for beating him so. Some others climbed to a bedroom window and grabbed the leg of a girlfriend to wake her, but got the wrong window and the wrong leg—both of them her father's!

Not all gangs value combat. But each will protect what it does value. When the retreatists find what they value threatened, they withdraw, protectively. When a conflict-oriented gang feels its status threatened, it fights.

"Status threat" is a special case of the general status thesis—that people will tend to do what gives them standing and respect in society. But with adolescent boys in a gang "what gives them standing and respect" is contained in the limited compass of the face-to-face relationships within the gang, not—except indirectly—with the social class structure of society at large. Of course, directly and indirectly, pressures from outside do affect the gang boys. They come from at least three levels.

Adult sponsored and controlled institutions of the larger society. Schools, places of employment, social agencies, police, and other officials represent adult "authority." Their orientation is middle-class; they preach and perhaps believe that worth and success come from hard work, deferred gratification, self control, good grades, good behavior, saving money, and becoming a "leader" in approved organizations. Gang boys fail to achieve according to these standards. The hypothesis that, with legitimate channels closed to them they will choose the illegitimate, therefore does not disagree with our findings. But precisely how this works is not very clear, and other research indicates that these boys may not be as alienated as many think. Other pressures must also affect them more directly.

The lower classes have their own adult community institutions, which make their own patterns and exert their own pressures. There are poolrooms, parties, informal neighborhood gatherings, and the obvious social and political power manifested by the adults in rackets and politics.

At this level, standards of adult behavior most appropriate to everyday life for the boys are inferred and directly inculcated. Observation strongly suggests that the gang boys recognize and respect the exercise of power in their neighborhoods, whether from legitimate or illegitimate sources. But there is no demonstration of legitimate power they know that compares in drama and impact with the evidence of the power of organized crime—the numerous gang slayings of hoodlums, and even of politicians. Both Negro and white gang boys repeat as a byword: "You can't beat the syndicate."

But modeling behavior after adults in order to "achieve adulthood" seems not to be as important a factor among Negroes as among whites. Lower-class Negro communities differ; there are fewer sharp age distinctions; all ages compete for excitement wherever it may be found—a bottle, a battle, or a broad. Poolhalls are frequented by young and old alike.

The adoption of adult lower-class standards therefore cannot be the only, or even the major, cause of delinquency among adolescents. In the conflict-prone gangs especially, the next level must be the most important.

The adolescent gang world. The juvenile "delinquent" —especially the gang leader—is faced with a condition, not a theory. He must daily act out his role under the eyes of his fellow gang members, and the members and leaders of other gangs. Almost by definition, the destiny of a warlike gang is controlled by the actions, real or expected, of other gangs. How a gang defends or enhances its status depends on its judgment of the whole fluid situation. What is the state of peace or war with rival gangs? What old gangs are feuding? What new gangs are trying to carve out niches for themselves?

Even a group organized for criminal purposes, as one of ours was, will shift its goals to fighting if under threat or attack from outside—even though this might, for a criminal gang, bring on risk of exposure.

The interrelationships in the gang world are extensive. A gang will have "branches" across neighborhood lines (East Side Cobras and West Side Cobras); it will have Senior, Junior, and Midget divisions within a neighborhood, with the younger members modeling themselves on the older, and expecting model behavior from them.

Even where pressures from outside make themselves manifest, they must filter down into and be expressed within the values of the gang itself. In fact the gang owes much of its reason for existence to its need to face and cope with such pressures, not losing status in the process —as would certainly happen if the adolescents had to face, nakedly, the censures, criticisms, and punishments of a middle-class or adult world they do not understand, and which does not understand them.

Each outside level represents forces which affect status within the gang—a boy can acquire "rep" by defiance of police, by vandalism of a neighborhood institution, or by showing "heart" in a gang fight. Whether or not the threat originated inside or outside the group, recognizing the existence of the gang and its internal dynamics is crucial to understanding how gang boys maintain status. The larger society is remote and abstract; even the neighborhood has indirect contact; the gang provides the face-to-face audience, the most direct and meaningful rewards and punishments.

Problems of status management are not confined to adolescent gangs. They affect us all—they rain on the just and the unjust alike, on parents, on delinquents, on corporation vice-presidents. And they rouse many besides juvenile gangs to violence.

In our work we noted that often merely assigning a worker to a gang, even before he had a chance to do anything, made the gang more docile, because being important enough to rate your own worker was such a mark of prestige that more energetic proof was not as necessary. Learning the techniques of status management—understanding the dynamics and importance of status considerations within juvenile gangs—provides a powerful lever by which gang behavior and delinquency can be grasped—and, perhaps, controlled.

September/October 1964

White Gangs

WALTER B. MILLER

If one thinks about street corner gangs at all these days, it is probably in the roseate glow of *West Side Story*, itself the last flowering of a literary and journalistic concern that goes back at least to the late 40's. Those were the days when it seemed that the streets of every city in the country had become dark battlefields where small armies of young men engaged their honor in terrible trials of combat, clashing fiercely and suddenly, then retiring to the warm succor of their girl cohorts. The forward to a 1958 collection of short stories, *The Young Punks,* captures a bit of the flavor:

> These are the stories behind today's terrifying headlines—about a strange new frightening cult that has grown up in our midst. Every writer whose work is included in this book tells the truth. These kids are tough. Here are knife-carrying killers, and thirteen-year-old street walkers who could give the most hardened call-

girl lessons. These kids pride themselves on their "ethics": never go chicken, even if it means knifing your own friend in the back. Never rat on a guy who wears your gang colors, unless he rats on you first. Old men on crutches are fair game. If a chick plays you for a sucker, blacken her eyes and walk away fast.

Today, the one-time devotee of this sort of stuff might be excused for wondering where they went, the Amboy Dukes and all those other adolescent warriors and lovers who so excited his fancy a decade ago. The answer, as we shall see, is quite simple—nowhere. The street gangs are still there, out on the corner where they always were.

The fact is that the urban adolescent street gang is as old as the American city. Henry Adams, in his *Education,* describes in vivid detail the gang fights between the Northsiders and Southsiders on Boston Common in the 1840's. An observer in 1856 Brooklyn writes: " . . . at any and all hours there are multitudes of boys . . . congregated on the corners of the streets, idle in their habits, dissolute in their conduct, profane and obscene in their conversation, gross and vulgar in their manners. If a female passes one of the groups she is shocked by what she sees and hears. . . . " The Red Raiders of Boston have hung out on the same corner at least since the 1930's; similarly, gang fighting between the Tops and Bottoms in West Philadelphia, which started in the 30's, is still continuing in 1969.

Despite this historical continuity, each new generation tends to perceive the street gang as a new phenomenon generated by particular contemporary conditions and destined to vanish as these conditions vanish. Gangs in the 1910's and 20's were attributed to the cultural dislocations and community disorganization accompanying the mass immigration of foreigners; in the 30's to the enforced idleness and economic pressures produced by the

Great Depression; in the 50's to the emotional disturbance of parents and children caused by the increased stresses and tensions of modern life. At present, the existence of gangs is widely attributed to a range of social injustices: racial discrimination, unequal educational and work opportunities, resentment over inequalities in the distribution of wealth and privilege in an affluent society, and the ineffective or oppressive policies of service agencies such as the police and the schools.

There is also a fairly substantial school of thought that holds that the street gangs are disappearing or have already disappeared. In New York City, the stage of so many real and fictional gang dramas of the 50's and early 60's, *The Times* sounded their death-knell as long ago as 1966. Very often, the passing of the gang is explained by the notion that young people in the slums have converted their gang-forming propensities into various substitute activities. They have been knocked out by narcotics, or they have been "politicized" in ways that consume their energies in radical or reform movements, or their members have become involved in "constructive" commercial activities, or enrolled in publicly financed education and/or work-training programs.

As has often been the case, these explanations are usually based on very shaky factual grounds and derived from rather parochial, not to say self-serving, perspectives. For street gangs are not only still widespread in United States cities, but some of them appear to have again taken up "gang warfare" on a scale that is equal to or greater than the phenomenon that received so much attention from the media in the 1950's.

In Chicago, street gangs operating in the classic formations of that city—War Lords, High Supremes, Cobra Stones—accounted for 33 killings and 252 injuries during the first six months of 1969. Philadelphia has experienced a wave of gang violence that has probably resulted in more murders in a shorter period of time than during any equivalent phase of the "fighting gang" era in New York. Police estimate that about 80 gangs comprising about 5,000 members are "active" in the city, and that about 20 are engaged in combat. Social agencies put the total estimated number of gangs at 200, with about 80 in the "most hostile" category. Between October 1962 and December 1968, gang members were reportedly involved in 257 shootings, 250 stabbings and 205 "rumbles." In the period between January 1968 and June 1969, 54 homicides and over 520 injuries were attributed to armed battles between gangs. Of the murder victims, all but eight were known to be affiliated with street gangs. The assailants ranged in age from 13 to 20, with 70 percent of them between 16 and 18 years old. Most of these gangs are designated by the name of the major corner where they hang out, the 12th and Poplar Streeters, or the 21 W's (for 21st and Westmoreland). Others bear traditional names such as the Centaurs, Morroccos and Pagans.

Gangs also continue to be active in Boston. In a single 90-minute period on May 10, 1969, one of the two channels of the Boston Police radio reported 38 incidents involving gangs, or one every 2½ minutes. This included two gang fights. Simultaneous field observation in several white lower-class neighborhoods turned up evidence that gangs were congregating at numerous street corners throughout the area.

Although most of these gangs are similar to the classic types to be described in what follows, as of this summer the national press had virtually ignored the revival of gang violence. *Time* magazine did include a brief mention of "casual mayhem" in its June 27 issue, but none of the 38 incidents in Boston on May 10 was reported even in the local papers. It seems most likely, however, that if all this had been going on in New York City, where most of the media have their headquarters, a spate of newspaper features, magazine articles and television "specials" would have created the impression that the country was being engulfed by a "new" wave of gang warfare. Instead, most people seem to persist in the belief that the gangs have disappeared or that they have been radically transformed.

This anomalous situation is partly a consequence of the problem of defining what a gang is (and we will offer a definition at the end of our discussion of two specific gangs), but it is also testimony to the fact that this enduring aspect of the lives of urban slum youth remains complex and poorly understood. It is hoped that the following examination of the Bandits and the Outlaws—both of Midcity—will clarify at least some of the many open questions about street corner gangs in American cities.

Midcity, which was the location of our 10-year gang study project (1954-64), is not really a city at all, but a portion of a large one, here called Port City. Midcity is a predominantly lower-class community with a relatively high rate of crime, in which both criminal behavior and a characteristic set of conditions—low-skill occupations, little education, low-rent dwellings, and many others—appeared as relatively stable and persisting features of a developed way of life. How did street gangs fit into this picture?

In common with most major cities during this period, there were many gangs in Midcity, but they varied widely in size, sex composition, stability and range of activities. There were about 50 Midcity street corners that served as hangouts for local adolescents. Fifteen of these were "major" corners, in that they were rallying points for the full range of a gang's membership, while the remaining 35 were "minor," meaning that in general fewer groups of smaller size habitually hung out there.

In all, for Midcity in this period, 3,650 out of 5,740, or 64 percent, of Midcity boys habitually hung out at a particular corner and could therefore be considered members of a particular gang. For girls, the figure is 1,125 out of 6,250, or 18 percent. These estimates also suggest that something like 35 percent of Midcity's boys, and 80 percent of its girls, did *not* hang out. What can be said about them? What made them different from the approximately 65 percent of the boys and 20 percent of the girls who did hang out?

Indirect evidence appears to show that the practice of hanging out with a gang was more prevalent among lower-status adolescents, and that many of those who were not known to hang out lived in middle-class or lower-class I (the higher range of the lower-class) areas. At the same time, however, it is evident that a fair proportion of higher-status youngsters also hung out. The question of status, and its relation to gang membership and gang behavior is very complex, but it should be borne in mind as we now take a closer look at the gangs we studied.

Between the Civil War and World War II, the Bandit neighborhood was well-known throughout the city as a colorful and close-knit community of Irish laborers. Moving to a flat in one of its ubiquitous three-decker frame tenements represented an important step up for the impoverished potato-famine immigrants who had initially settled in the crowded slums of central Port City. By the 1810's the second generation of Irish settlers had produced a spirited and energetic group of athletes and politicos, some of whom achieved national prominence.

Those residents of the Bandit neighborhood who shared in some degree the drive, vitality and capability of these famous men assumed steady and fairly remunerative positions in the political, legal and civil service world of Port City, and left the neighborhood for residential areas whose green lawns and single houses represented for them what Midcity had represented for their fathers and grandfathers. Those who lacked these qualities remained in the Bandit neighborhood, and at the outset of World War II made up a stable and relatively homogeneous community of low-skilled Irish laborers.

The Bandit neighborhood was directly adjacent to Midcity's major shopping district, and was spotted with bars, poolrooms and dance halls that served as meeting places for an active neighborhood social life. Within two blocks of the Bandits' hanging-out corner were the Old Erin and New Hibernia dance halls, and numerous drinking establishments bearing names such as the Shamrock, Murphy and Donoghue's, and the Emerald Bar and Grill.

A number of developments following World War II disrupted the physical and social shape of the Bandit community. A mammoth federally-financed housing project sliced through and blocked off the existing network of streets and razed the regular rows of wooden tenements. The neighborhood's small manufacturing plants were progressively diminished by the growth of a few large establishments, and by the 1950's the physical face of the neighborhood was dominated by three large and growing plants. As these plants expanded they bought off many of the properties which had not been taken by the housing project, demolished buildings, and converted them into acres of black-topped parking lots for their employees.

During this period, the parents of the Bandit corner gang members stubbornly held on to the decreasing number of low-rent, deteriorating, private dwelling units. Although the Bandits' major hanging corner was almost surrounded by the housing project, virtually none of the gang members lived there. For these families, residence in the housing project would have entailed a degree of financial stability and restrained behavior that they were unable or unwilling to assume, for the corner gang members of the Bandit neighborhood were the scions of men and women who occupied the lowest social level in Midcity. For them low rent was a passion, freedom to drink and to behave drunkenly a sacred privilege, sporadic employment a fact of life, and the social welfare and law-enforcement agencies of the state, partners of one's existence.

The Bandit Corner was subject to field observation for about three years—from June 1954 to May 1957. Hanging out on the corner during this period were six distinct but related gang subdivisions. There were four male groups: The Brigands, aged approximately 18 to 21 at the start of the study period; the Senior Bandits, aged 16 to 18; the Junior Bandits, 14 to 16, and the Midget Bandits, 12 to 14. There were also two distinct female subdivisions: The Bandettes, 14 to 16, and the Little Bandettes, 12 to 14.

The physical and psychic center of the Bandit corner was Sam's Variety Store, the owner and sole employee of which was not Sam but Ben, his son. Ben's father had founded the store in the 1920's, the heyday of the Irish laboring class in the Bandit neighborhood. When his father died, Ben took over the store, but did not change its name. Ben was a stocky, round-faced Jew in his middle 50's, who looked upon the whole of the Bandit neighborhood as his personal fief and bounden responsibility—a sacred legacy from his father. He knew everybody and was concerned with everybody; through his store passed a constant stream of customers and noncustomers of all ages and both sexes. In a space not much larger than that of a fair-sized bedroom Ben managed to crowd a phone booth, a juke box, a pinball machine, a space heater, counters, shelves and stock, and an assorted variety of patrons. During one 15-minute period on an average day Ben would supply $1.37 worth of groceries to 11-year-old Carol Donovan and enter the sum on her mother's page in the "tab" book, agree to extend Mrs. Thebodeau's already extended credit until her A.D.C. check arrived, bandage and solace the three-year-old Negro girl who came crying to him with a cut forefinger, and shoo into the street a covey of Junior Bandits whose altercation over a pinball score was impeding customer traffic and augmenting an already substantial level of din.

Ben was a bachelor, and while he had adopted the whole of the Bandit neighborhood as his extended family, he had taken on the 200 adolescents who hung out on the Bandit corner as his most immediate sons and daughters. Ben knew the background and present circumstances of every Bandit, and followed their lives with intense interest and concern. Ben's corner-gang progeny were a fast-moving and mercurial lot, and he watched over their adventures and misadventures with a curious mixture of indignation, solicitude, disgust, and sympathy. Ben's outlook on the affairs of the world was never bland; he held and freely voiced strong opinions on a wide variety of issues, prominent among which was the behavior and misbehavior of the younger generation.

This particular concern was given ample scope for attention by the young Bandits who congregated in and around his store. Of all the gangs studied, the Bandits were the most consistently and determinedly criminal, and central to Ben's concerns was how each one stood with regard to "trouble." In this respect, developments were seldom meager. By the time they reached the age of 18, every one of the 32 active members of the Senior Bandits had appeared in court at least once, and some many times; 28 of the 32 boys had been committed to a correctional institution and 16 had spent at least one term in confinement.

Ben's stout arm swept the expanse of pavement which fronted his store. "I'll tell ya, I give up on these kids. In all the years I been here, I never seen a worse bunch. You know what they should do? They should put up a big platform with one of them stocks right out there, and as soon as a kid gets in trouble, into the stocks with 'im. Then they'd straighten out. The way it is now, the kid tells a sob story to some soft-hearted cop or social worker, and pretty soon he's back at the same old thing. See that guy just comin' over here? That's what I mean. He's hopeless. Mark my word, he's gonna end up in the electric chair."

The Senior Bandit who entered the store came directly to Ben. "Hey, Ben, I just quit my job at the shoe factory. They don't pay ya nothin', and they got some wise guy nephew of the owner who thinks he can kick everyone around. I just got fed up. I ain't gonna tell Ma for awhile, she'll be mad." Ben's concern was evident. "Digger, ya just gotta learn you can't keep actin' smart to every boss ya have. And $1.30 an hour ain't bad pay at all for a 17-year-old boy. Look, I'll lend ya 10 bucks so ya can give 5 to ya Ma, and she won't know."

In their dealings with Ben, the Bandits, for their part, were in turn hostile and affectionate, cordial and sullen, open and reserved. They clearly regarded Ben's as "their" store. This meant, among other things, exclusive possession of the right to make trouble within its confines. At least three times during the observation period corner boys from outside neighborhoods entered the store obviously bent on stealing or creating a disturbance. On each occasion these outsiders were efficiently and forcefully removed by nearby

Bandits, who then waxed indignant at the temerity of "outside" kids daring to consider Ben's as a target of illegal activity. One consequence, then, of Ben's seigneurial relationship to the Bandits was that his store was unusually well protected against theft, armed and otherwise, which presented a constant hazard to the small-store owner in Midcity.

On the other hand, the Bandits guarded jealously their own right to raise hell in Ben's. On one occasion, several Senior Bandits came into the store with a cache of pistol bullets and proceeded to empty the powder from one of the bullets onto the pinball machine and to ignite the powder. When Ben ordered them out they continued operations on the front sidewalk by wrapping gunpowder in newspaper and igniting it. Finally they set fire to a wad of paper containing two live bullets which exploded and narrowly missed local residents sitting on nearby doorsteps.

Such behavior, while calculated to bedevil Ben and perhaps to retaliate for a recent scolding or ejection, posed no real threat to him or his store; the same boys during this period were actively engaged in serious thefts from similar stores in other neighborhoods. For the most part, the behavior of the Bandits in and around the store involved the characteristic activities of hanging out. In warm weather the Bandits sat outside the store on the sidewalk or doorstoops playing cards, gambling, drinking, talking to one another and to the Bandettes. In cooler weather they moved into the store as the hour and space permitted, and there played the pinball machine for such cash payoffs as Ben saw fit to render, danced with the Bandettes to juke box records, and engaged in general horseplay.

While Ben's was the Bandits' favorite hangout, they did frequent other hanging locales, mostly within a few blocks of the corner. Among these was a park directly adjacent to the housing project where the boys played football and baseball in season. At night the park provided a favored locale for activities such as beer drinking and lovemaking, neither of which particularly endeared them to the adult residents of the project, who not infrequently summoned the police to clear the park of late-night revellers. Other areas of congregation in the local neighborhood were a nearby delicatessen ("the Delly"), a pool hall, and the apartments of those Bandettes whose parents happened to be away. The Bandits also ran their own dances at the Old Erin and New Hibernia, but they had to conceal their identity as Bandits when renting these dance halls, since the proprietors had learned that the rental fees were scarcely sufficient to compensate for the chaos inevitably attending the conduct of a Bandit dance.

The Bandits were able to find other sources of entertainment in the central business district of Port City. While most of the Bandits and Bandettes were too young to gain admission to the numerous downtown cafes with their rock 'n' roll bands, they were able to find amusement in going to the movies (sneaking in whenever possible), playing the coin machines in the penny arcades and shoplifting from the downtown department stores. Sometimes, as a kind of diversion, small groups of Bandits spent the day in town job-hunting, with little serious intention of finding work.

One especially favored form of downtown entertainment was the court trial. Members of the Junior and Senior Bandits performed as on-stage participants in some 250 court trials during a four-year period. Most trials involving juveniles were conducted in nearby Midcity Court as private proceedings, but the older Bandits had adopted as routine procedure the practice of appealing their local court sentences to the Superior Court located in downtown

Port City. When the appeal was successful, it was the occasion for as large a turnout of gang members as could be mustered, and the Bandits were a rapt and vitally interested audience. Afterwards, the gang held long and animated discussions about the severity or leniency of the sentence and other, finer points of legal procedure. The hearings provided not only an absorbing form of free entertainment, but also invaluable knowledge about court functioning, appropriate defendant behavior, and the predilections of particular judges—knowledge that would serve the spectators well when their own turn to star inevitably arrived.

The Senior Bandits, the second oldest of the four male gang subdivisions hanging out on the Bandit corner, were under intensive observation for a period of 20 months. At the start of this period the boys ranged in age from 15 to 17 (average age 16.3) and at the end, 17 to 19 (average age 18.1). The core group of the Senior Bandits numbered 32 boys.

Most of the gang members were Catholic, the majority of Irish background; several were Italian or French Canadian, and a few were English or Scotch Protestants. The gang contained two sets of brothers and several cousins, and about one third of the boys had relatives in other subdivisions. These included a brother in the Midgets, six brothers in the Juniors, and three in the Marauders.

The educational and occupational circumstances of the Senior Bandits were remarkably like those of their parents. Some seven years after the end of the intensive study period, when the average age of the Bandits was 25, 23 out of the 27 gang members whose occupations were known held jobs ordinarily classified in the bottom two occupational categories of the United States census. Twenty-one were classified as "laborer," holding jobs such as roofer, stock boy, and trucker's helper. Of 24 fathers whose occupations were known, 18, or 83 percent, held jobs in the same bottom two occupational categories as their sons; 17 were described as "laborer," holding jobs such as furniture mover and roofer. Fathers even held jobs of similar kinds and in similar proportions to those of their sons, e.g., construction laborers: sons 30 percent, fathers 25 percent; factory laborers: sons 15 percent, fathers 21 percent. Clearly the Senior Bandits were not rising above their fathers' status. In fact, there were indications of a slight decline, even taking account of the younger age of the sons. Two of the boys' fathers held jobs in "public safety" services—one policeman and one fireman; another had worked for a time in the "white collar" position of a salesclerk at Sears; a fourth had risen to the rank of Chief Petty Officer in the Merchant Marine. Four of the fathers, in other words, had attained relatively elevated positions, while the sons produced only one policeman.

The education of the Senior Bandits was consistent with their occupational status. Of 29 boys whose educational experience was known, 27 dropped out of school in the eighth, ninth, or tenth grades, having reached the age of 16. Two did complete high school, and one of these was reputed to have taken some post-high-school training in a local technical school. None entered college. It should be remarked that this record occurred not in a backward rural community of the 1800's, nor in a black community, but in the 1950's in a predominantly white neighborhood of a metropolis that took pride in being one of the major educational centers of the world.

Since only two of the Senior Bandits were still in school during the study, almost all of the boys held full-time jobs at some time during the contact period. But despite financial needs, pressure from parents and parole officers and other incentives to get work, the Senior Bandits found jobs slowly, accepted them reluctantly, and quit them with little provocation.

The Senior Bandits were clearly the most criminal of the seven gangs we studied most closely. For example, by the time he had reached the age of 18 the average Senior Bandit had been charged with offenses in court an average of 7.6 times; this compared with an average rate of 2.7 for all five male gangs, and added up to a total of almost 250 separate charges for the gang as a whole. A year after our intensive contact with the group, 100 percent of the Senior Bandits had been arrested at least once, compared with an average arrest figure of 45 percent for all groups. During the 20-month contact period, just about half of the Senior Bandits were on probation or parole for some period of time.

To a greater degree than in any of the other gangs we studied, crime as an occupation and preoccupation played a central role in the lives of the Senior Bandits. Prominent among recurrent topics of discussion were thefts successfully executed, fights recently engaged in, and the current status of gang members who were in the process of passing through the successive states of arrest, appearing in court, being sentenced, appealing, re-appealing and so on. Although none of the crimes of the Senior Bandits merited front-page headlines when we were close to them, a number of their more colorful exploits did receive newspaper attention, and the stories were carefully clipped and left in Ben's store for circulation among the gang members. Newspaper citations functioned for the Senior Bandits somewhat as do press notices for actors; gang members who made the papers were elated and granted prestige; those who did not were often disappointed; participants and non-participants who failed to see the stories felt cheated.

The majority of their crimes were thefts. The Senior Bandits were thieves *par excellence,* and their thievery was imaginative, colorful, and varied. Most thefts were from stores. Included among these was a department store theft of watches, jewelry and clothing for use as family Christmas presents; a daylight raid on a supermarket for food and refreshments needed for a beach outing; a daytime burglary of an antique store, in which eight gang members, in the presence of the owner, stole a Samurai sword and French duelling pistols. The gang also engaged in car theft. One summer several Bandits stole a car to visit girl friends who were working at a summer resort. Sixty miles north of Port City, hailed by police for exceeding speed limits, they raced away at speeds of up to 100 miles an hour, overturned the car, and were hospitalized for injuries. In another instance, Bandits stole a car in an effort to return a drunken companion to his home and avoid the police; when this car stalled they stole a second one parked in front of its owner's house; the owner ran out and fired several shots at the thieves, which, however, failed to forestall the theft.

The frequency of Senior Bandit crimes, along with the relative seriousness of their offenses, resulted in a high rate of arrest and confinement. During the contact period somewhat over 40 percent of the gang members were confined in correctional institutions, with terms averaging 11 months per boy. The average Senior Bandit spent approximately one month out of four in a correctional facility. This circumstance prompted one of the Bandettes to remark, "Ya know, them guys got a new place to hang—the reformatory. That bunch is never together—one halfa them don't even know the other half. . . . "

This appraisal, while based on fact, failed to recognize an important feature of gang relationships. With institutional confinement a frequent and predictable event, the Senior Bandits employed a set of devices to maintain a high degree of group solidarity. Lines of communication between corner and institution were kept open by frequent visits by those on the outside, during which inmates were brought food, money and cigarettes as well as news of the neighborhood and other correctional facilities. One Mid-city social worker claimed that the institutionalized boys knew what was going on in the neighborhood before most neighborhood residents. The Bandits also developed well-established methods for arranging and carrying out institutional escape by those gang members who were so inclined. Details of escapes were arranged in the course of visits and inter-inmate contacts; escapees were provided by fellow gang members with equipment such as ropes to scale prison walls and getaway cars. The homes of one's gang fellows were also made available as hideouts. Given this set of arrangements, the Bandits carried out several highly successful escapes, and one succeeded in executing the first escape in the history of a maximum security installation.

The means by which the Senior Bandits achieved group cohesion in spite of recurrent incarcerations of key members merit further consideration—both because they are of interest in their own right, and because they throw light on important relationships between leadership, group structure, and the motivation of criminal behavior. Despite the assertion that "one halfa them guys don't know the other half," the Senior Bandits were a solidaristic associational unit, with clear group boundaries and definite criteria for differentiating those who were "one of us" from those who were not. It was still said of an accepted group member that "he hangs with us"—even when the boy had been away from the corner in an institution for a year or more.

Incarcerated leaders, in particular, were referred to frequently and in terms of admiration and respect.

The system used by the Senior Bandits to maintain solidarity and reliable leadership arrangements incorporated three major devices: the diffusion of authority, anticipation of contingencies, and interchangeability of roles. The recurring absence from the corner of varying numbers of gang members inhibited the formation of a set of relatively stable cliques of the kind found in the other gangs we studied intensively. What was fairly stable, instead, was a set of "classes" of members, each of which could include different individuals at different times. The relative size of these classes was fairly constant, and a member of one class could move to another to take the place of a member who had been removed by institutionalization.

The four major classes of gang members could be called key leaders, standby leaders, primary followers, and secondary followers. During the intensive contact period the gang contained five key leaders—boys whose accomplishments had earned them the right to command; six standby leaders—boys prepared to step into leadership positions when key leaders were institutionalized; eight primary followers—boys who hung out regularly and who were the most dependable followers of current leaders; and 13 secondary followers—boys who hung out less regularly and who tended to adapt their allegiances to particular leadership situations.

Predictably, given the dominant role of criminal activity among the Senior Bandits, leadership and followership were significantly related to criminal involvement. Each of the five key leaders had demonstrated unusual ability in criminal activity; in this respect the Senior Bandits differed from the other gangs, each of which included at least one leader whose position was based in whole or in part on a commitment to a law-abiding course of action. One of the Senior Bandits' key leaders was especially respected for his daring and adeptness in theft; another, who stole infrequently relative to other leaders, for his courage, stamina and resourcefulness as a fighter. The other three leaders had proven themselves in both theft and fighting, with theft the more important basis of eminence.

Confinement statistics show that gang members who were closest to leadership positions were also the most active in crime. They also suggest, however, that maintaining a system of leadership on this basis poses special problems. The more criminally active a gang member, the greater the likelihood that he would be apprehended and removed from the neighborhood, thus substantially diminishing his opportunities to convert earned prestige into operative leadership. How was it possible, then, for the Senior Bandits to maintain effective leadership arrangements? They utilized a remarkably efficient system whose several features were ingenious and deftly contrived.

First, the recognition by the Bandits of five key leaders—a relatively large number for a gang of 32 members—served as a form of insurance against being left without leadership. It was most unlikely that all five would be incarcerated at the same time, particularly since collective crimes were generally executed by one or possibly two leaders along with several of their followers. During one relatively brief part of the contact period, four of the key leaders were confined simultaneously, but over the full period the average number confined at any one time was two. One Bandit key leader expressed his conviction that exclusive reliance on a single leader was unwise: " . . . since we been hangin' out [at Ben's corner] we ain't had no leader. Other kids got a leader of the gang. Like up in Cornerville, they always got one kid who's the big boss . . . so far we ain't did that, and I don't think we ever will. We talk about 'Smiley and his boys,' or 'Digger and his clique,' and like that. . . . "

It is clear that for this Bandit the term "leader" carried the connotation of a single and all-powerful gang lord, which was not applicable to the diffuse and decentralized leadership arrangements of the Bandits. It is also significant that the gangs of Cornerville which he used as an example were Italian gangs whose rate of criminal involvement was relatively low. The "one big boss" type of leadership found in these gangs derives from the "Caesar" or "Il Duce" pattern so well established in Italian culture, and it was workable for Cornerville gangs because the gangs and their leaders were sufficiently law-abiding and/or sufficiently capable of evading arrest as to make the removal of the leader an improbable event.

A second feature of Bandit leadership, the use of "standby" leaders, made possible a relatively stable balance among the several cliques. When the key leader of his clique was present in the area, the standby leader assumed a subordinate role and did not initiate action; if and when the key leader was committed to an institution, the standby was ready to assume leadership. He knew, however, that he was expected to relinquish this position on the return of the key leader. By this device each of the five major cliques was assured some form of leadership even when key leaders were absent, and could maintain its form, identity and influence vis-a-vis other cliques.

A third device that enabled the gang to maintain a relatively stable leadership and clique structure involved the phenomenon of "optimal" criminal involvement. Since excellence in crime was the major basis of gang leadership, it might be expected that some of those who aspired to leadership would assume that there was a simple and direct relationship between crime and leadership: the more crime, the more prestige; the more prestige, the stronger the basis of authority. The flaw in this simple formula was in fact recognized by the actual key leaders: in striving for maximal criminal involvement, one also incurred the maximum risk of incarceration. But leadership involved more than gaining prestige through crime; one had to be personally involved with other gang members for sufficiently extended periods to exploit won prestige through wooing followers, initiating noncriminal as well as criminal activities, and effecting working relationships with other leaders. Newly-returned key leaders as well as the less criminally-active class of standby leaders tended to step up their involvement in criminal activity on assuming or reassuming leadership positions in order to solidify their positions, but they also tended to diminish such involvement once this was achieved.

One fairly evident weakness in so flexible and fluid a system of cliques and leadership was the danger that violent and possibly disruptive internal conflict might erupt among key leaders who were competing for followers, or standby leaders who were reluctant to relinquish their positions. There was, in fact, surprisingly little overt conflict of any kind among Bandit leaders. On their release from confinement, leaders were welcomed with enthusiasm and appropriate observances both by their followers and by other leaders. They took the center of the stage as they recounted to rapt listeners their institutional experiences, the circumstances of those still confined, and new developments in policies, personnel and politics at the correctional school.

When they were together Bandit leaders dealt with one another gingerly, warily and with evident respect. On one occasion a standby leader, who was less criminally active than the returning key leader, offered little resistance to being displaced, ·but did serve his replacement with the warning that a resumption of his former high rate of crime would soon result in commitment both of himself and his clique. On another occasion one of the toughest of the Senior Bandits (later sentenced to an extended term in an adult institution for ringleading a major prison riot), returned to the corner to find that another leader had taken over not only some of his key followers but his steady girl friend as well. Instead of taking on his rival in an angry and perhaps violent confrontation, he reacted quite mildly, venting his hostility in the form, of sarcastic teasing, calculated to needle but not to incite. In the place of a direct challenge, the newly returned key leader set about to regain his followers and his girl by actively throwing himself back into criminal activity. This course of action—competing for followers by successful performance in prestigious activities rather than by brute-force confrontation—was standard practice among the Senior Bandits.

The leadership system of the Junior Bandits was, if anything, even farther removed from the "one big boss" pattern than was the "multi-leader power-balance" system of the Seniors. An intricate arrangement of cliques and leadership enabled this subdivision of the gang to contain within it a variety of individuals and cliques with different and often conflicting orientations.

Leadership for particular activities was provided as the occasion arose by boys whose competence in that activity had been established. Leadership was thus flexible, shifting, and adaptable to changing group circumstances. Insofar as there was a measure of relatively concentrated authority, it was invested in a collectivity rather than an individual. The several "situational" leaders of the dominant clique constituted what was in effect a kind of ruling council, which arrived at its decisions through a process of extended collective discussion generally involving all concerned. Those who were to execute a plan of action thereby took part in the process by which it was developed.

A final feature of this system concerns the boy who was recognized as "the leader" of the Junior Bandits. When the gang formed a club to expedite involvement in athletic activities, he was chosen its president. Although he was an accepted member of the dominant clique, he did not, on the surface, seem to possess any particular qualifications for this position. He was mild-mannered, unassertive, and consistently refused to take a definite stand on outstanding issues, let alone taking the initiative in implementing policy. He appeared to follow rather than to lead. One night when the leaders of the two subordinate factions became infuriated with one another in the course of a dispute, he trailed both boys around for several hours, begging them to calm down and reconcile their differences. On another occasion the gang was on the verge of splitting into irreconcilable factions over a financial issue. One group accused another of stealing club funds; the accusation was hotly denied; angry recriminations arose that swept in a variety of dissatisfactions with the club and its conduct. In the course of this melee, the leader of one faction, the "bad boys," complained bitterly about the refusal of the president to take sides or assume any initiative in resolving the dispute, and called for a new election. This was agreed to and the election was held—with the result that the "weak" president was re-elected by a decisive majority, and was reinstated in office amidst emotional outbursts of acclaim and reaffirmation of the unity of the gang.

It was thus evident that the majority of gang members, despite temporary periods of anger over particular issues, recognized on some level the true function performed by a "weak" leader. Given the fact that the gang included a set of cliques with differing orientations and conflicting notions, and a set of leaders whose authority was limited to specific areas, the maintenance of gang cohesion required some special mechanisms. One was the device of the "weak" leader. It is most unlikely that a forceful or dominant person could have controlled the sanctions that would enable him to coerce the strong-willed factions into compliance. The very fact that the "weak" leader refused to take sides and was noncommittal on key issues made him acceptable to the conflicting interests represented in the gang. Further, along with the boy's nonassertive demeanor went a real talent for mediation.

The Outlaw street corner was less than a mile from that of the Bandits, and like the Bandits, the Outlaws were white, Catholic, and predominantly Irish, with a few Italians and Irish-Italians. But their social status, in the middle range of the lower class, was sufficiently higher than that of the Bandits to be reflected in significant differences in both their gang and family life. The neighborhood environment also was quite different.

Still, the Outlaws hung out on a classic corner—complete with drug store, variety store, a neighborhood bar (Callahan's Bar and Grill), a pool hall, and several other small businesses such as a laundromat. The corner was within one block of a large park, a convenient locale for card games, lovemaking, and athletic practice. Most residents of the Outlaw neighborhood were oblivious to the deafening roar of the elevated train that periodically rattled the houses and stores of Midcity Avenue, which formed one street of the Outlaw corner. There was no housing project in the Outlaw neighborhood, and none of the Outlaws were project residents. Most of their families rented one level of one of the three-decker wooden tenements which were common in the area; a few owned their own homes.

In the mid-1950's, however, the Outlaw neighborhood underwent significant changes as Negroes began moving in. Most of the white residents, gradually and with reluctance, left their homes and moved out to the first fringe of Port City's residential suburbs, abandoning the area to the Negroes.

Prior to this time the Outlaw corner had been a hanging locale for many years. The Outlaw name and corner dated from at least the late 1920's, and perhaps earlier. One local boy who was not an Outlaw observed disgruntledly that anyone who started a fight with an Outlaw would end up fighting son, father, and grandfather, since all were or had been members of the gang. A somewhat drunken and sentimental Outlaw, speaking at a farewell banquet for their field worker, declared impassionedly that any infant born into an Outlaw family was destined from birth to wear the Outlaw jacket.

One consequence of the fact that Outlaws had hung out on the same corner for many years was that the group that congregated there during the 30-month observation period included a full complement of age-graded subdivisions. Another consequence was that the subdivisions were closely connected by kinship. There were six clearly differentiated subdivisions on the corner: the Marauders, boys in their late teens and early twenties; the Senior Outlaws, boys between 16 and 18; the Junior Outlaws, 14 to 16; and the Midget Outlaws, 11 to 13. There were also two girls groups, the Outlawettes and the Little Outlawettes. The number of Outlaws in all subdivisions totalled slightly over 200 persons, ranging in age, approximately, from 10 to 25 years.

The cohesiveness of the Outlaws, during the 1950's, was enhanced in no small measure by an adult who, like Ben for the Bandits, played a central role in the Outlaws' lives. This was Rosa—the owner of the variety store which was their principal hangout—a stout, unmarried woman of about 40 who was, in effect, the street-corner mother of all 200 Outlaws.

The Junior Outlaws, numbering 24 active members, were the third oldest of the four male subdivisions on the Outlaw Corner, ranging in age from 14 to 16. Consistent with their middle-range lower-class status, the boys' fathers were employed in such jobs as bricklayer, mechanic, chauffeur, milk deliveryman; but a small minority of these men had attained somewhat higher positions, one being the owner of a small electroplating shop and the other rising to the position of plant superintendent. The educational status of the Junior Outlaws was higher than that of the Bandit gangs, but lower than that of their older brother gang, the Senior Outlaws.

With regard to law violations, the Junior Outlaws, as one might expect from their status and age, were considerably less criminal than the lower-status Bandits, but considerably more so than the Senior Outlaws. They ranked third among the five male gangs in illegal involvement during the observation period (25 involvements per 10 boys per 10 months), which was well below the second-ranking Senior Bandits (54.2) and well above the fourth-ranking Negro Kings (13.9). Nevertheless, the two-and-a-half-year period during which we observed the Juniors was for them, as for other boys of their status and age group, a time of substantial increase in the frequency and seriousness of illegal behavior. An account of the events of this time provides some insight into the process by which age-related influences engender criminality. It also provides another variation on the issue, already discussed in the case of the Bandits, of the relation of leadership to criminality.

It is clear from the case of the Bandits that gang affairs were ordered not by autocratic ganglords, but rather through a subtle and intricate interplay between leadership and a set of elements such as personal competency, intra-gang divisions and law violation. The case of the Junior Outlaws is particularly dramatic in this regard, since the observation period found them at the critical age when boys of this social-status level are faced with a serious decision— the amount of weight to be granted to law-violating behavior as a basis of prestige. Because there were in the Junior Outlaws two cliques, each of which was committed quite clearly to opposing alternatives, the interplay of the various elements over time emerges with some vividness, and echoes the classic morality play wherein forces of good and evil are locked in mortal combat over the souls of the uncommitted.

At the start of the observation period, the Juniors, 13-, 14- and 15-year-olds, looked and acted for the most part like "nice young kids." By the end of the period both their voices and general demeanor had undergone a striking change. Their appearance, as they hung out in front of Rosa's store, was that of rough corner boys, and the series of thefts, fights and drinking bouts which had occurred during the intervening two-and-one-half years was the substance behind that appearance. When we first contacted them, the Juniors comprised three main cliques; seven boys associated primarily with a "good boy" who was quite explicitly oriented to law-abiding behavior; a second clique of seven boys associated with a "bad boy" who was just starting to pursue prestige through drinking and auto theft; and a third, less-frequently congregating group, who took a relatively neutral position with respect to the issue of violative behavior.

The leader of the "good boy" clique played an active

part in the law-abiding activities of the gang, and was elected president of the formal club organized by the Juniors. This club at first included members of all three cliques; however, one of the first acts of the club members, dominated by the "good boy" leader and his supporters, was to vote out of membership the leader of the "bad boy" clique. Nevertheless, the "bad boy" leader and his followers continued to hang out on the corner with the other Juniors, and from this vantage point attempted to gain influence over the uncommitted boys as well as members of the "good boy" clique. His efforts proved unsuccessful, however, since during this period athletic prowess served for the majority of the Juniors as a basis of greater prestige than criminal behavior. Disgruntled by this failure, the "bad boy" leader took his followers and moved to a new hanging corner, about two blocks away from the traditional one.

From there, a tangible symbol of the ideological split within the Juniors, the "bad boy" leader continued his campaign to wean away the followers of the "good boy" leader, trying to persuade them to leave the old corner for the new. At the same time, behavior at the "bad boy" corner became increasingly delinquent, with, among other things, much noisy drinking and thefts of nearby cars. These incidents produced complaints by local residents that resulted in several police raids on the corner, and served to increase the antagonism between what now had become hostile factions. Determined to assert their separateness, the "bad boy" faction began to drink and create disturbances in Rosa's store, became hostile to her when she censured them, and finally stayed away from the store altogether.

The antagonism between the two factions finally became sufficiently intense to bring about a most unusual circumstance—plans for an actual gang fight, a "jam" of the type characteristic of rival gangs. The time and place for the battle were agreed on. But no one from either side showed up. A second battle site was selected. Again the combatants failed to appear. From the point of view of intragang relations, both the plan for the gang fight and its failure to materialize were significant. The fact that a physical fight between members of the same subdivision was actually projected showed that factional hostility over the issue of law violation had reached an unusual degree of bitterness; the fact that the planned encounters did not in fact occur indicated a realization that actual physical combat might well lead to an irreversible split.

A reunification of the hostile factions did not take place for almost a year, however. During this time changes occurred in both factions which had the net effect of blunting the sharpness of the ideological issue dividing them. Discouraged by his failure to win over the majority of the Outlaws to the cause of law-violation as a major badge of prestige, the leader of the "bad boy" clique began to hang out less frequently. At the same time, the eight "uncommitted" members of the Junior Outlaws, now moving toward their middle teens, began to gravitate toward the "bad boy" corner—attracted by the excitement and risk of its activities. More of the Juniors than ever before became involved in illegal drinking and petty theft. This trend became sufficiently pronounced to draw in members of the "good boy" clique, and the influence of the "good boy" leader diminished to the point where he could count on the loyalty only of his own brother and two other boys. In desperation, sensing the all-but-irresistible appeal of illegality for his erstwhile followers, he increased the tempo of his own delinquent behavior in a last-ditch effort to win them back. All in vain. Even his own brother deserted the regular Outlaw corner, although he did not go so far as to join the "bad boys" on theirs.

Disillusioned, the "good boy" leader took a night job that sharply curtailed the time he was able to devote to gang activities. Members of the "bad boy" clique now began a series of maneuvers aimed at gaining control of the formal club. Finally, about two months before the close of the 30-month contact period, a core member of the "bad boy" clique was elected to the club presidency. In effect, the proponents of illegality as a major basis of prestige had won the long struggle for dominance of the Junior Outlaws. But this achievement, while on the surface a clear victory for the "bad boy" faction, was in fact a far more subtle process of mutual accommodation.

The actions of each of the opposing sides accorded quite directly with their expressed convictions; each member of the "bad boy" faction averaged about 17 known illegal acts during the observation period, compared to a figure of about two per boy for the "good boy" faction. However, in the face of these sharp differences in both actions and sentiments respecting illegality, the two factions shared important common orientations. Most importantly, they shared the conviction that the issue of violative behavior as a basis of prestige was a paramount one, and one that required a choice. Moreover, both sides remained uncertain as to whether the choice they made was the correct one.

The behavior of both factions provides evidence of a fundamental ambivalence with respect to the "demanded" nature of delinquent behavior. The gradual withdrawal of support by followers of the "good boy" leader and the movement toward violative behavior of the previously "neutral" clique attest to a compelling conviction that prestige gained through law-abiding endeavor alone could not, at this age, suffice. Even more significant was the criminal experience of the "good boy" leader. As the prime exponent of law-abiding behavior, he might have been expected to serve as an exemplar in this respect. In fact, the opposite was true; his rate of illegal involvement was the highest of all the boys in his clique, and had been so even before his abortive attempt to regain his followers by a final burst of delinquency. This circumstance probably derived from his realization that a leader acceptable to both factions (which he wanted to be) would have to show proficiency in activities recognized by both as conferring prestige.

It is equally clear, by the same token, that members of the "bad boy" faction were less than serenely confident in their commitment to law-violation as an ideal. Once they had won power in the club they did not keep as their leader the boy who had been the dominant figure on the "bad boy" corner, and who was without question the most criminally active of the Junior Outlaws, but instead elected as president another boy who was also criminally active, but considerably less so. Moreover, in the presence of older gang members, Seniors and Marauders, the "bad boy" clique was far more subdued, less obstreperous, and far less ardent in their advocacy of crime as an ideal. There was little question that they were sensitive to and responsive to negative reactions by others to their behavior.

It is noteworthy that members of both factions adhered more firmly to the "law-violation" and "law-abiding" positions on the level of abstract ideology than on the level of actual practice. This would suggest that the existence of the opposing ideologies and their corresponding factions served important functions both for individual gang members and for the group as a whole. Being in the same orbit as the "bad boys" made it possible for the "good boys" to reap some of the rewards of violative behavior without undergoing its risks; the presence of the "good boys" imposed restraints on the "bad" that they themselves desired, and helped protect them from dangerous excesses. The behavior and ideals of the "good boys" satisfied for both factions that component of their basic orientation that said "violation of the law is wrong and should be punished;" the behavior and ideals of the "bad boys" that component that said "one cannot earn manhood without some involvement in criminal activity."

It is instructive to compare the stress and turmoil attending the struggle for dominance of the Junior Outlaws with the leadership circumstances of the Senior Bandits. In this gang, older and of lower social status (lower-class III), competition for leadership had little to do with a choice between law-abiding and law-violating philosophies, but rather with the issue of which of a number of competing leaders was *best* able to demonstrate prowess in illegal activity. This virtual absence of effective pressures against delinquency contrasts sharply with the situation of the Junior Outlaws. During the year-long struggle between its "good" and "bad" factions, the Juniors were exposed to constant pressures, both internal and external to the gang, to refrain from illegality. External sources included Rosa, whom the boys loved and respected; a local youth worker whom they held in high esteem; their older brother gangs, whose frequent admonitions to the "little kids" to "straighten out" and "keep clean" were attended with utmost seriousness. Within the gang itself the "good boy" leader served as a consistent and persuasive advocate of a law-abiding course of action. In addition, most of the boys' parents deplored their misbehavior and urged them to keep out of trouble.

In the face of all these pressures from persons of no small importance in the lives of the Juniors, the final triumph of the proponents of illegality, however tempered, assumes added significance. What was it that impelled the "bad boy" faction? There was a quality of defiance about much of their delinquency, as if they were saying—"We know perfectly well that what we are doing is regarded as wrong, legally and morally; we also know that it violates the wishes and standards of many whose good opinion we value; yet, if we are to sustain our self-respect and our honor as males we *must*, at this stage of our lives, engage in criminal behavior." In light of the experience of the Junior Outlaws, one can scarcely argue that their delinquency sprang from any inability to distinguish right from wrong, or out of any simple conformity to a set of parochial standards that just happened to differ from those of the legal code or the adult middle class. Their delinquent behavior was engendered by a highly complex interplay of forces, including, among other elements, the fact that they were males, were in the middle range of the lower class and of critical importance in the present instance, were moving through the age period when the attainment of manhood was of the utmost concern.

In the younger gang just discussed, the Junior Outlaws, leadership and clique structure reflected an intense struggle between advocates and opponents of law-violation as a prime basis of prestige.

Leadership in the older Senior Outlaws reflected a resolution of the law-conformity versus law-violation conflict, but with different results. Although the gang was not under direct observation during their earlier adolescence, what we know of the Juniors, along with evidence that the Senior Outlaws themselves had been more criminal when younger, would suggest that the gang had in fact undergone a similar struggle, and that the proponents of conformity to the law had won.

In any case, the events of the observation period made it

clear that the Senior Outlaws sought "rep" as a gang primarily through effective execution of legitimate enterprises such as athletics, dances, and other non-violative activities. In line with this objective, they maintained a consistent concern with the "good name" of the gang and with "keeping out of trouble" in the face of constant and ubiquitous temptations. For example, they attempted (without much success) to establish friendly relations with the senior priest of their parish—in contrast with the Junior Outlaws, who were on very bad terms with the local church. At one point during the contact period when belligerent Bandits, claiming that the Outlaws had attacked one of the Midget Bandits, vowed to "wipe out every Outlaw jacket in Midcity," the Senior Outlaws were concerned not only with the threat of attack but also with the threat to their reputation. "That does it," said one boy, "I knew we'd get into something. There goes the good name of the Outlaws."

Leadership and clique arrangements in the Senior Outlaws reflected three conditions, each related in some way to the relatively low stress on criminal activity: the stability of gang membership (members were rarely removed from the area by institutional confinement), the absence of significant conflict over the prestige and criminality issue, and the importance placed on legitimate collective activities. The Senior Bandits were the most unified of the gangs we observed directly; there were no important cleavages or factions; even the distinction between more-active and less-active members was less pronounced than in the other gangs.

But as in the other gangs, leadership among the Senior Outlaws was collective and situational. There were four key leaders, each of whom assumed authority in his own sphere of competence. As in the case of the Bandit gangs there was little overt competition among leaders; when differences arose between the leadership and the rank and file, the several leaders tended to support one another. In one significant respect, however, Outlaw leadership differed from that of the other gangs; authority was exercised more firmly and accepted more readily. Those in charge of collective enterprises generally issued commands after the manner of a tough army sergeant or work-gang boss. Although obedience to such commands was frequently less than flawless, the leadership style of Outlaw leaders approximated the "snap-to-it" approach of organizations that control firmer sanctions than do most corner gangs. Compared to the near-chaotic behavior of their younger brother gang, the organizational practices of the Senior appeared as a model of efficiency. The "authoritarian" mode of leadership was particularly characteristic of one boy, whose prerogatives were somewhat more generalized than those of the other leaders. While he was far from an undisputed "boss," holding instead a kind of *primus inter pares* position, he was as close to a "boss" as anything found among the direct-observation gangs.

His special position derived from the fact that he showed superior capability in an unusually wide range of activities, and this permitted him wider authority than the other leaders. One might have expected, in a gang oriented predominantly to law-abiding activity, that this leader would serve as an exemplar of legitimacy and rank among the most law-abiding. This was not the case. He was, in fact, one of the most criminal of the Senior Outlaws, being among the relatively few who had "done time." He was a hard drinker, an able street-fighter, a skilled football strategist and team leader, an accomplished dancer and smooth ladies' man. His leadership position was based not on his capacity to best exemplify the law-abiding orientation of the gang, but on his capabilities in a variety of activities, violative and non-violative. Thus, even in the gang most concerned with "keeping clean," excellence in crime still constituted one important basis of prestige. Competence as such rather than the legitimacy of one's activities provided the major basis of authority.

We still have to ask, however, why leadership among the Senior Outlaws was more forceful than in the other gangs. One reason emerges by comparison with the "weak leader" situation of the Junior Bandits. Younger and of lower social status, their factional conflict over the law-violation-and-prestige issue was sufficiently intense so that only a leader without an explicit commitment to either side could be acceptable to both. The Seniors, older and of higher status, had developed a good degree of intragang consensus on this issue, and showed little factionalism. They could thus accept a relatively strong leader without jeopardizing gang unity.

A second reason also involves differences in age and social status, but as these relate to the world of work. In contrast to the younger gangs, whose perspectives more directly revolved around the subculture of adolescence and its specific concerns, the Senior Outlaws at age 19 were on the threshold of adult work, and some in fact were actively engaged in it. In contrast to the lower-status gangs whose orientation to gainful employment was not and never would be as "responsible" as that of the Outlaws, the activities of the Seniors as gang members more directly reflected and anticipated the requirements and conditions of the adult occupational roles they would soon assume.

Of considerable importance in the prospective occupational world of the Outlaws was, and is, the capacity to give and take orders in the execution of collective enterprises. Unlike the Bandits, few of whom would ever occupy other than subordinate positions, the Outlaws belonged to that sector of society which provides the men who exercise direct authority over groups of laborers or blue collar workers. The self-executed collective activities of the gang—organized athletics, recreational projects, fund-raising activities—provided a training ground for the practice of organizational skills—planning organized enterprises, working together in their conduct, executing the directives of legitimate superiors. It also provided a training ground wherein those boys with the requisite talents could learn and practice the difficult art of exercising authority effectively over lower-class men. By the time they had reached the age of 20, the leaders of the Outlaws had experienced in the gang many of the problems and responsibilities confronting the army sergeant, the police lieutenant and the factory foreman.

The nature and techniques of leadership in the Senior Outlaws had relevance not only to their own gang but to the Junior Outlaws as well. Relations between the Junior and Senior Outlaws were the closest of all the intensive-contact gang subdivisions. The Seniors kept a close watch on their younger fellows, and served them in a variety of ways, as athletic coaches, advisers, mediators and arbiters. The older gang followed the factional conflicts of the Juniors with close attention, and were not above intervening when conflict reached sufficient intensity or threatened their own interests. The dominant leader of the Seniors was particularly concerned with the behavior of the Juniors; at one point, lecturing them about their disorderly conduct in Rosa's store, he remarked, "I don't hang with you guys, but I know what you do. . . . " The Seniors did not, however, succeed in either preventing the near-break-up of the Junior Outlaws or slowing their move toward law-breaking activities.

The subtle and intricately contrived relations among

cliques, leadership and crime in the four subdivisions of the
Bandits and Outlaws reveal the gang as an ordered and adaptive form of association, and its members as able and rational human beings. The fascinating pattern of intergang variation within a basic framework illustrates vividly the compelling influences of differences in age and social status on crime, leadership and other forms of behavior—even when these differences are surprisingly small. The experiences of Midcity gang members show that the gang serves the lower-class adolescent as a flexible and adaptable training instrument for imparting vital knowledge concerning the value of individual competence, the appropriate limits of law-violating behavior, the uses and abuses of authority, and the skills of interpersonal relations. From this perspective, the street gang appears not as a casual or transient manifestation that emerges intermittently in response to unique and passing social conditions, but rather as a stable associational form, coordinate with and complementary to the family, and as an intrinsic part of the way of life of the urban low-status community.

How then can one account for the widespread conception of gangs as somehow popping up and then disappearing again? One critical reason concerns the way one defines what a gang is. Many observers, both scholars and non-scholars, often use a *sine qua non* to sort out "real" gangs from near-gangs, pseudo-gangs, and non-gangs. Among the more common of these single criteria are: autocratic one-man leadership, some "absolute" degree of solidarity or stable membership, a predominant involvement in violent conflict with other gangs, claim to a rigidly defined turf, or participation in activities thought to pose a threat to other sectors of the community. Reaction to groups lacking the *sine qua non* is often expressed with a dismissive "Oh, them. That's not a *gang*. That's just a bunch of kids out on the corner."

For many people there are no gangs if there is no gang warfare. It's that simple. For them, as for all those who concentrate on the "threatening" nature of the gang, the phenomenon is defined in terms of the degree of "problem" it poses: A group whose "problematic" behavior is hard to ignore is a gang; one less problematic is not. But what some people see as a problem may not appear so to others. In Philadelphia, for example, the police reckoned there were 80 gangs, of which 20 were at war; while social workers estimated there were 200 gangs, of which 80 were "most hostile." Obviously, the social workers' 80 "most hostile" gangs were the same as the 80 "gangs" of the police. The additional 120 groups defined as gangs by the social workers were seen as such because they were thought to be appropriate objects of social work; but to the police they were not sufficiently troublesome to require consistent police attention, and were not therefore defined as gangs.

In view of this sort of confusion, let me state our definition of what a gang is. A gang is a group of urban adolescents who congregate recurrently at one or more nonresidential locales, with continued affiliation based on self-defined criteria of inclusion and exclusion. Recruitment, customary places of assembly and ranging areas are based in a specific territory, over some portion of which limited use and occupancy rights are claimed. Membership both in the gang as a whole and in its subgroups is determined on the basis of age. The group maintains a versatile repertoire of activities, with hanging out, mating, recreational and illegal activity being of central importance; and it is internally differentiated on the basis of authority, prestige, personality and clique-formation.

The main reason that people have consistently mistaken the prevalence of gangs is the widespread tendency to define them as gangs on the basis of the presence or absence of one or two characteristics that are thought to be essential to the "true" gang. Changes in the forms or frequencies or particular characteristics, such as leadership, involvement in fighting, or modes of organization, are seen not as normal variations over time and space, but rather as signs of the emergence or disappearance of the gangs themselves. Our work does not support this view; instead, our evidence indicates that the core characteristics of the gang vary continuously from place to place and from time to time without negating the existence of the gang. Gangs may be larger or smaller, named or nameless, modestly or extensively differentiated, more or less active in gang fighting, stronger or weaker in leadership, black, white, yellow or brown, without affecting their identity as gangs. So long as groups of adolescents gather periodically outside the home, frequent a particular territory, restrict membership by age and other criteria, pursue a variety of activities, and maintain differences in authority and prestige—so long will the gang continue to exist as a basic associational form.

September 1969

FURTHER READING SUGGESTED BY THE AUTHOR:

The Gang: A Study of 1313 Gangs in Chicago by Frederic M. Thrasher (Chicago: University of Chicago Press, 1927) is the classic work on American youth gangs. Although published in the 1920's, it remains the most detailed and comprehensive treatise on gangs and gang life ever written.

Delinquent Boys: The Culture of the Gang by Albert K. Cohen (Glencoe, Ill.: Free Press, 1955) is the first major attempt to explain the behavior of gang members using modern sociological theory.

Delinquency and Opportunity: A Theory of Delinquent Gangs by Richard A. Cloward and Lloyd E. Ohlin (Glencoe, Ill.: Free Press, 1960) explains the existence, both of gangs, and major types of gangs. It has had a profound impact on American domestic policy.

Group Process and Gang Delinquency by James F. Short Jr. and Fred L. Strodtbeck (Chicago: University of Chicago Press, 1965). An empirical "test" of divergent theories of gangs and delinquency, it includes the first extensive application of statistical techniques and the first systematic application of the social-psychological conceptual framework to the study of gangs.

Crime, Victims, and the Police

PHILLIP ENNIS

"A skid row drunk lying in a gutter is crime. So is the killing of an unfaithful wife. A Cosa Nostra conspiracy to bribe public officials is crime. So is a strong-arm robbery...." So states the report of the President's Commission on Law Enforcement and Administration of Justice, commonly known as the Crime Commission report, in pointing out the diversity of crime. Our recent investigation at Chicago's National Opinion Research Center reveals that Americans are also frequent prey to incidents which may not fall firmly within the jurisdiction of criminal law, but which still leave the ordinary citizen with a strong sense of victimization—consumer frauds, landlord-tenant violations, and injury or property damage due to someone else's negligent driving.

With the aid of a new research method for estimating national crime rates the Crime Commission study has now confirmed what many have claimed all along—that the rates for a wide range of personal crimes and property offenses are considerably higher than previous figures would indicate. Traditional studies have relied on the police blotter for information. The present research, devised and carried out by the National Opinion Research Center (NORC), tried a survey approach instead. Taking a random sample of 10,000 households during the summer of 1965, we asked people what crimes had been committed against them during the preceding year. The results—roughly 2,100 verified incidents—indicated that as many as half of the people interviewed were victims of offenses which they did not report to the police.

This finding raised several questions. How much did this very high incidence of unreported offenses alter the picture presented by the standard measures, notably the FBI's Uniform Crime Reports (UCR) index, based only on reported incidents? What was the situation with minor offenses, those not considered in the UCR index? What sorts of crimes tended to go unreported? And why did so many victims fail to contact the authorities? These were some of the issues we attempted to probe.

More than 20 percent of the households surveyed were criminally victimized during the preceding year. This figure includes about *twice as much* major crime as reported by the UCR index. The incidence of minor crimes—simple assaults, petty larcenies, malicious mischiefs, frauds, and so on —is even greater. According to our research, these are at least twice as frequent as major crimes. The UCR index includes seven major crimes, so the proliferation of petty offenses not taken into account by the index makes the discrepancy between that index and the real crime picture even greater than a consideration of major offenses alone would indicate.

Table I compares our figures with the UCR rates for the

seven major crimes upon which the index is based—homicide, forcible rape, robbery, aggravated assault, burglary, larceny (over $50), and auto theft. The homicide rate projected by the survey is very close to the UCR rate—not surprising since murder is the crime most likely to be discovered and reported.

TABLE I—ESTIMATED RATES OF MAJOR CRIMES: 1965-1966

Crime	NORC sample: estimated rate per 100,000	Uniform Crime Reports, 1965: individual or residential rates per 100,000
Homicide	3.0	5.1
Forcible rape	42.5	11.6
Robbery	94.0	61.4*
Aggravated assault	218.3	106.6
Burglary	949.1	296.6*
Larceny ($50+)	606.5	267.4*
Car theft	206.2	226.0†
Total	2,119.6	974.7

* The 1965 Uniform Crime Reports show for burglary and larcenies the number of residential and individual crimes. The overall rate per 100,000 population is therefore reduced by the proportion of these crimes that occurred to individuals. Since all robberies to individuals were included in the NORC sample regardless of whether the victim was acting as an individual or as part of an organization, the *total* UCR figure was used for comparison.

† The reduction of the UCR auto theft rate by 10 percent is based on the figures of the Automobile Manufacturers Association, showing that 10 percent of all cars are owned by leasing-rental agencies and private and governmental fleets. The Chicago Police Department's auto theft personnel confirmed that about 7-10 percent of stolen cars recovered were from fleet, rental, and other non-individually owned sources.

The survey estimate of the car theft rate is puzzlingly low. This could be because people report their cars "stolen" to the police and then find that they themselves have "misplaced" the car or that someone else has merely "borrowed" it. They may either forget the incident when interviewed or be too embarrassed to mention it. The relatively high rate of auto thefts reported to the police confirms other studies which show people are more likely to notify the police in this case than they are if they are victims of most other crimes. It may also indicate that people think the police can or will do more about a car theft than about many other offenses.

The startling frequency of reported forcible rape, four times that of the UCR index, underscores the peculiar nature of this crime. It occurs very often among people who know each other—at the extreme, estranged husband and wife—and there appears to be some stigma attached to the victim. Yet among the cases discovered in the survey, too few to be statistically reliable, most were reported to the police. Do the police tend to downgrade the offense into an assault or a minor sex case or put it into some miscellaneous category? This is a well-known practice for certain other kinds of crime.

To what extent is crime concentrated in the urban environment? To what extent are there regional differences in crime rates? And to what extent are the poor, and especially Negroes, more or less likely to be victims of crime? Behind these questions lie alternative remedial measures, measures which range from city planning and antipoverty programs to the training and organization of police departments and the allocation of their resources throughout the nation.

The NORC findings presented in Figure I give an overview of the crime rates for central cities in metropolitan areas, for their suburban environs, and for nonmetropolitan areas in the four main regions of the country. The chart shows the crime rate (per 100,000 population) for serious crimes against the person (homicide, rape, robbery, and

Figure I—

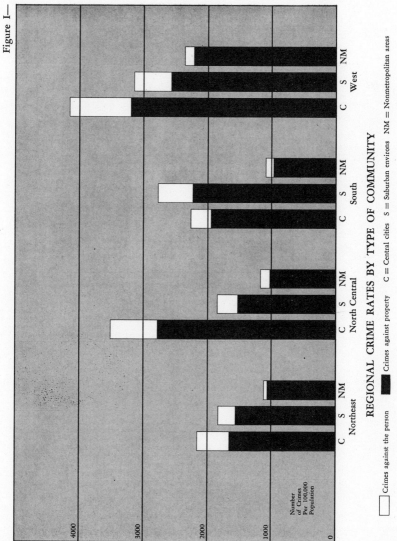

REGIONAL CRIME RATES BY TYPE OF COMMUNITY

☐ Crimes against the person ■ Crimes against property C = Central cities S = Suburban environs NM = Nonmetropolitan areas

aggravated assault) and serious crimes against property (burglary, larceny over $50, and vehicle theft).

The myth of the wild West is borne out by our figures. Its present crime rate, for both property and personal crimes, is higher than that of any other region of the country. The West has almost twice the rates of the Northeast for all three types of communities. The South, in contrast, does not appear to have the high rate of violent crime that is sometimes alleged.

As one moves from the central city to the suburbs and out into the smaller towns and rural areas, the crime rates decline, but much more drastically for crimes against the person than for property crimes. The metropolitan center has a violent crime rate about *five times* as high as the smaller city and rural areas, but a property crime rate only *twice* as high.

Evidently the city is a more dangerous place than the suburbs or a small town. Yet these figures require some qualification: About 40 percent of the aggravated assaults and rapes (constituting most of the serious crimes against the person) take place *within* the victim's home; and about 45 percent of all the serious crimes against the person are committed by someone familiar to the victim. Random "crime in the streets" by strangers is clearly *not* the main picture that emerges from these figures, even in the urban setting.

Who are the victims? Among lower income groups (under $6,000 per year) Negroes are almost twice as likely as whites to be victims of serious crimes of violence but only very slightly more likely to be victims of property crimes. Our figures show that, per 100,000 population, an estimated 748 low-income Negroes per year will be victims of criminal violence and 1,927 victims of property offenses, whereas the numbers for whites in the same income bracket are

402 and 1,829. The situation is exactly reversed for upper income groups. The wealthier Negro is not much more likely than the white to be a victim of a violent crime, but he is considerably more likely to have property stolen. His chances of losing property are 3,024 in 100,000, whereas the figure is only 1,765 for whites in the same income bracket. Burglary is the most common property crime against more affluent Negroes. The implication is that ghetto neighborhoods in which poor and richer Negroes live side by side make the latter more valuable to property losses than are higher income whites, who can live in more economically homogeneous areas.

Despite the fact then that per capita offense rates are generally acknowledged to be higher among Negroes than among whites, the incidence of whites being victimized by Negroes—an image frequently conjured up by the specter of "crime in the streets"—is relatively infrequent. Negroes tend instead to commit offenses against members of their own race. The same is true of whites. Further, to the extent that crime is interracial at all, Negroes are more likely to be victims of white offenders than vice versa. Our figures show that only 12 percent of the offenses against whites in our sample were committed by nonwhites, whereas 19 percent of the nonwhite victims reported that the persons who committed offenses against them were white.

What happens when a person is victimized? How often are law enforcement and judicial authorities involved? What changes occur in the victim's attitude and behavior as a result of the incident?

If the "right thing" to do is to call the police when you have been a victim of a crime, and there is considerable pressure to do just that, why is it that half the victimizations were not reported to the police?

The more serious the crime, the more likely it is to be

reported: 65 percent of the aggravated assaults in our sample were reported to the police, but only 46 percent of the simple assaults; 60 percent of the grand larcenies, but only 37 percent of the petty larcenies. Insurance recovery also appears to play a role in the very high rate of reported auto thefts (89 percent) and reported victimizations that are the result of automobile negligence (71 percent). Victims of offenses at the border of the criminal law apparently do not think the police should be involved. Only 10 percent of the consumer fraud victims called the police, whereas 26 percent of the ordinary fraud victims (mainly those of bad checks) did so.

Those victims who said they did not notify the police were asked why. Their reasons fell into four fairly distinct categories. The first was the belief that the incident was not a police matter. These victims (34 percent) did not want the offender to be harmed by the police or thought that the incident was a private, not a criminal, affair. Two percent of the nonreporting victims feared reprisal, either physically from the offender's friends or economically from cancellation of or increases in rates of insurance. Nine percent did not want to take the time or trouble to get involved with the police, did not know whether they should call the police, or were too confused to do so. Finally, a substantial 55 percent of the nonreporting victims failed to notify the authorities because of their attitudes toward police effectiveness. These people believed the police could not do anything about the incident, would not catch the offenders, or would not want to be bothered.

The distribution of these four types of reasons for failure to notify police varies by type of crime and by the social characteristics of the victim, but two points are clear. First, there is strong resistance to invoking the law enforcement process even in matters that are clearly criminal. Second, there is considerable skepticism as to the effectiveness of police action.

A clue to this skepticism lies in the events which follow a call to the police. All the victims who reported an offense were asked how the police reacted and how far the case proceeded up the judicial ladder—arrest, trial, sentencing, and so forth. We have simplified the process into six stages:

■ Given a "real" victimization, the police were or were not notified.

■ Once notified, the police either came to the scene of the victimization (or in some other way acknowledged the event) or failed to do so.

■ Once they arrived, the police did or did not regard the incident as a crime.

■ Regarding the matter as a crime, the police did or did not make an arrest.

■ Once an arrest was made, there was or was not a trial (including plea of guilty).

■ The outcome of the trial was to free the suspect (or punish him "too leniently") or to find him guilty and give him the "proper" punishment.

Figure II shows the tremendous attrition as the cases proceed from the bottom of the "iceberg," the initial victimization, to the top, the trial and sentencing. Failure of the police to heed a call and their rejection of the incident as a crime account for a large proportion of this attrition. Also noteworthy are the low arrest and trial rates. Once the offender is brought to trial, however, the outcome appears more balanced. About half the offenders were treated too leniently in the victim's view, but the other half were convicted and given "proper" punishment.

How do the victims feel about this truncated legal process? Do they feel that the situation is their own fault and

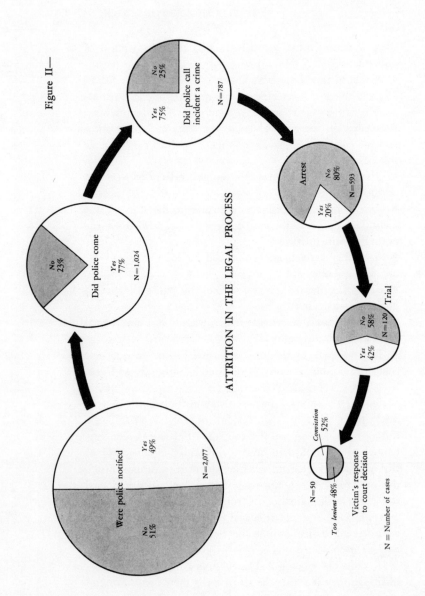

Figure II—

ATTRITION IN THE LEGAL PROCESS

Did police call
incident a crime
No 25%
Yes 75%
N=787

Did police come
No 23%
Yes 77%
N=1,024

Arrest
No 80%
Yes 20%
N=593

Trial
No 58%
Yes 42%
N=120

Were police notified
Yes 49%
No 51%
N=2,077

Victim's response
to court decision
Conviction 52%
Too lenient 48%
N=50

N = Number of cases

accept it, or are they dissatisfied with the relatively frequent failure of the police to apprehend the offender? When the victims were asked their feelings about the outcome of the incident, only 18 percent said they were very satisfied; another 19 percent were somewhat satisfied; 24 percent were somewhat dissatisfied; and 35 percent were very dissatisfied (4 percent gave no answer).

The level of satisfaction was closely related to how far the case went judicially. (See Table II.) People who did not call the police at all were the most dissatisfied. If they called and the police did not come, about the same percentage were very dissatisfied; but peculiarly, there were more who reported that they were satisfied. An· arrest lowered the dissatisfaction level, but the dramatic differences appeared when the offender was brought to trial. If he was acquitted or given too lenient a penalty (in the victim's view), dissatisfaction ran high; if he was convicted and given the "proper" penalty, the victim was generally quite pleased. This suggests that the ordinary citizen's sense of justice includes a vengeful element—a desire for punishment over and above monetary compensation for loss. Advocates of rehabilitation rather than retribution for criminals might well take such public sentiments into account.

Quite independent of the judicial outcome of the case is its impact on the daily life and feelings of the victim and his family. Slightly more than 40 percent of the victims reported increased suspicion and distrustfulness along with intensified personal and household security measures. It appears that it is the unpredictability of the event and the sense of invasion by strangers rather than the seriousness of the crime that engenders this mistrust. With these strong feelings and the frequent lack of knowledge about the identity of the offender, victimization may well

TABLE II—DEGREE OF SATISFACTION WITH OUTCOME OF OFFENSE

Disposition of case	Very satisfied	Somewhat satisfied	Somewhat dissatisfied	Very dissatisfied
No notification of police	13%	18%	28%	41%
Police did not respond to notification	22	22	18	38
Police did not consider incident a crime	24	26	24	26
Crime, but no arrest	20	23	27	30
Arrest, but no trial	33	21	22	24
Acquittal or too lenient penalty	17	13	26	44
Conviction and "proper" penalty	60	16	12	12

exacerbate existing prejudice against the groups typically blamed for social disorder and crime.

How does the public feel about the police? The survey asked all the crime victims and a comparably large sample of nonvictims a series of questions probing their attitudes on how well the local police do their job, how respectful they are toward the citizenry, and how honest they are. Items concerning the limits of police authority and exploring the functions of the police were also included.

Several conclusions emerged. Upper income groups are consistently more favorable in their evaluation of the police and are more in favor of augmenting their power than those with lower incomes. Negroes at all income levels show strong negative attitudes toward the police. (See Tables III and IV.)

Table III shows rather clearly that Negroes, regardless of income, estimate police effectiveness lower than whites do, with Negro women being even more critical than Negro men of the job the police are doing. Furthermore, Negroes show a smaller shift in attitude with increasing income than do whites, who are more favorable in their opinion of police effectiveness as their income rises.

TABLE III—POSITIVE OPINIONS ON LOCAL POLICE EFFECTIVENESS

(Percentage who think police do an excellent or good job in enforcing the law)

	White		Nonwhite	
Sex	Less than $6,000	$6,000 or more	Less than $6,000	$6,000 or more
Male	67%	72%	54%	56%
Female	66	74	39	43

Table IV shows that Negroes are also sharply more critical than whites are of police honesty. Here there are no income differences in attitude among white males. Women at higher income levels, both white and Negro, appear to be relatively less suspicious of police honesty. It is difficult to say how much these attitude differences are attributable to actual experience with police corruption and how much they express degrees of general hostility to the police. In either case the results indicate a more negative attitude toward the police among Negroes than among whites.

TABLE IV—OPINIONS ON THE HONESTY OF NEIGHBORHOOD POLICE

	Males			
	White		Nonwhite	
Police are . . .	Less than $6,000	$6,000 or more	Less than $6,000	$6,000 or more
Almost all honest	65%	67%	33%	33%
Most honest, few corrupt	24	26	47	41
Almost all corrupt	3	1	9	19
Don't know	8	6	11	7

	Females			
	White		Nonwhite	
Police are . . .	Less than $6,000	$6,000 or more	Less than $6,000	$6,000 or more
Almost all honest	57%	65%	24%	35%
Most honest, few corrupt	27	29	54	49
Almost all corrupt	2	0	10	4
Don't know	14	6	12	12

The next question probed a more personal attitude toward the police—their respectfulness toward "people like yourself." Almost 14 percent of the Negroes answered that it was "not so good." Less than 3 percent of the whites chose this response. This represents a much more critical attitude by Negroes than by whites, with hardly any differences by sex or income. There is some tendency, however, for very low income people of both races and sexes to feel that the police are not sufficiently respectful to them. One further conclusion is more tentative. It appears that there is no *one* underlying attitude toward the police. The police have many and sometimes only slightly related jobs to do in society. For example, they have a role both in suppressing organized gambling and in maintaining civil order. Most people (73 percent) feel the police should stop gambling even though it brings a good deal of money into the community. A significant minority (21 percent) feel the police should act only on complaints, and only 2 percent said the police should not interfere with gambling at all. With respect to police control of demonstrations for civil and political rights, on the other hand, a slight majority (54 percent) say police should not interfere if the protests are peaceful; 40 percent say police should stop all demonstrations; and 3 percent feel demonstrations should be allowed under any and all circumstances. Negroes are much more permissive about demonstrations than whites, and somewhat more permissive about gambling. Among lower income Negroes there is a significant relation between permissiveness on gambling and a strong prodemonstration attitude. But whites show no such consistent attitudes on the two issues. They tend to favor police intervention in gambling but not in rights demonstrations.

A more dramatic example of discontinuities in attitudes toward police has to do with limitations on their power. A national cross-section of citizens was asked:

■ "Recently some cities have added civilian review boards to their police departments. Some people say such boards offer the public needed protection against the police, and others say these boards are unnecessary and would interfere with good police work and morale. In general, would you be in favor of civilian review boards or opposed to them?"

In favor _____ 45%
Opposed _____ 35
Don't know _____ 20

■ "Do you favor giving the police more power to question people, do you think they have enough power already, or would you like to see some of their power to question people curtailed?"

Police should have more power _____ 52%
Have enough power already _____ 43
Should curtail power _____ 5

■ "The police sometimes have a hard time deciding if there is enough evidence to arrest a suspect. In general, do you think it is better for them to risk arresting an innocent person rather than letting the criminal get away, or is it better for them to be really sure they are getting the right person before they make an arrest?"

Risk arresting innocent _____ 42%
Be really sure _____ 58

■ "The Supreme Court has recently ruled that in criminal cases the police may not question a suspect without his lawyer being present, unless the suspect agrees to be questioned without a lawyer. Are you in favor of this Supreme Court decision or opposed to it?"

In favor _____ 65%
Opposed _____ 35

The significance of these results is their lack of consensus. On none of the questions is there overwhelming agreement or disagreement. Opinions are split almost in half, with the exception that hardly anyone is in favor of curtailing present police powers. The advocates of extending police authority in questioning suspects are almost balanced by those who think the police have enough power to do their job. Further, there is lack of internal agreement on the specific facets of the question. Being in favor of a civilian review board does not necessarily make a person support the Supreme Court decision on interrogation of suspects. Nor does a preference for having the police risk arresting the innocent rather than letting a criminal go free strongly predict being in favor of granting more power to the police in questioning people.

It is not clear why attitudes toward the police are so scattered. Perhaps police power is too new an issue on the national scene to have its components hammered into a clear and cohesive whole. Local variations in police practices may also blur the situation. It appears we are only at the beginning of a long process of relocating the police in the political spectrum.

As the federal presence in local law enforcement enlarges, both the shape of crime and the nature of law enforcement itself will change. Accurate crime statistics will be essential in monitoring these changes and in evaluating the worth of new programs designed to protect the public from the growing threat of invasion and victimization by criminal acts.

June 1967

FURTHER READING SUGGESTED BY THE AUTHOR:

The Challenge of Crime in a Free Society (Washington, D.C.: United States Government Printing Office). A report by the President's Commission on Law Enforcement and Administration of Justice.

The American Jury by Harry Kalven, Jr. and Hans Zeisel (Boston: Little, Brown and Company, 1966).

Arrest edited by Wayne R. LaFave (Boston: Little, Brown and Company, 1965). The report of the American Bar Foundation's Survey of the Administration of Criminal Justice in the United States.

The Respectable Criminal

DONALD R. CRESSEY

Spring has returned, and with it two of the major themes of strategy in American life—how to win a baseball pennant and how to beat the income tax collector. Because as a sociologist I'm professionally interested in why people cheat, I'll leave theories about baseball to others.

At this time of year many of us toy with the idea of income tax evasion. Some succumb to the temptation. Those who do are not poor, culturally deprived slum dwellers. They do not like to think of themselves as "criminals." Tax evaders, along with people who pad their insurance claims, embezzle from their employers, or conspire with others to fix the price of goods usually have steady jobs and wear white collars to work. They are, nevertheless, committing what we call "respectable crimes." As recurrent newspaper headlines remind us, these are widespread forms of criminal behavior in our society. To develop a truly comprehensive theory of criminality we must learn more about why such men become violators of the law.

My own interest in "respectable crime" goes back to my days as a graduate student at Indiana University after World War II. My major professor, Edwin H. Sutherland, was conducting a study of the crimes committed by the 70 largest non-financial corporations in the U.S. He invented the concept of white-collar crime and encouraged criminologists, administrators of criminal justice, and laymen to re-examine the generalizations they had traditionally made about crime and criminals.

Sutherland's examination of the laws on certain kinds of business practices—such as restraint of trade, infringement of patents, false and misleading advertising, unfair labor practices—convinced him that these were indeed criminal laws. Violation of these laws is, accordingly, a crime; crimes of this sort must be included in any generalization about crimes and criminals. Sutherland found that the 70 largest corporations had about 980 decisions recorded against them for violation of four laws—an average of about 14 for each corporation. At the time of the study, the most popular criminological theories tended to link criminal behavior to social and personal pathologies of various kinds. Theoreticians emphasized poverty, poor education, broken homes, and psychological characteristics of criminals. The white-collar criminals that Sutherland had discovered, like the high officials of G.E. and Westinghouse who were convicted of conspiracy to fix prices in 1962, were persons of respectability and high social status who had committed crimes in connection with business. They did not fit the theoretical description. It followed that the theory would have to be revised to account for this type of criminality.

Sutherland's position was confused by the fact that he studied corporations, rather than individual white-collar criminals. I tried to correct this defect by making a study of embezzlers. It was my impression that embezzlers are white-collar criminals whose backgrounds are not likely to contain the social and personal pathologies which popular notions and traditional theory ascribe to criminals. Actually I doubt that these characteristics are in fact present in the background of *most* criminals. On the basis of my study, I *know* that they are almost never present in the background of embezzlers.

When I turned, as a first step, to the existing literature for an explanation of embezzling, I found that there was a basic confusion about the nature of this crime. Most books about embezzling are written by accountants—guides to businessmen to help them avoid embezzling in their own firms. Their major thesis is that weak internal controls and poor auditing systems cause defalcations by failing to eliminate the possibility of committing the crime.

While I must agree that a detailed check on all business transactions would prevent defalcations, I doubt whether these crimes can be "explained" by the absence of such checks. In the first place, even the most "foolproof" accounting procedures can never eliminate cheating entirely. The versatility of embezzlers is astounding, and greatly underestimated. In the second place, modern society presupposes business transactions based upon a considerable amount of trust. No matter what accounting system is used, an element of trust remains. A brief review of the history of embezzlement as a crime will make this point clear.

When commerce was beginning to expand in the 16th century, the legal rule regarding financial relations between master, servants, and third persons was simply this: (a) property received from the master remained in his possession, the servant having "mere charge or custody" of it; but (b) property received from a third person for the master *was* in the *servant's* possession, and he was not guilty of a felony if he converted it for his own use. As business expanded and "servants" became in fact clerks and cashiers, the situations in which the master retained possession were expanded. It became the rule that if a clerk placed money in a cash drawer, it thereby came into the possession of the master; if the servant subsequently took the money from the cash drawer to keep, this act was larceny. But until 1799, if a clerk received money from one of his employer's customers and *put it directly into his own pocket,* he had committed no crime; the money had not yet come into his employer's possession. Later that same year the first general embezzlement statute was passed in England. The new law covered "servants" but it did not cover "agents"; when in 1812 a stockbroker took money given to him to invest and converted it for his own uses, the court held that the general embezzlement law did not cover this act. New legislation to cover brokers, agents, etc., was passed almost immediately. Clearly, the common law of fraud and larceny had been sufficient for a relatively simple economy where there was no need to trust servants with business transactions. But with the growth of business firms in the 19th century, embezzlement statutes had to be invented to cover the new offenses which arose with the new economic structure.

Dependence upon trusted employees, agents, brokers, and factors has increased steadily since the passage of these first statutes. To argue that criminal violation of financial trust can be prevented by rigid accounting methods is to overlook the pertinent point: if strict controls were imposed on all trusted persons, embezzlement could be prevented, but very little business could be conducted. To remove "the temptation, the opportunity, and even the suggestion to violate the solemn trust which has been placed in officers and

employees," as one accountant-author suggests, would eliminate both "solemn trust" and large numbers of business
transactions.

Writers who are not accountants have an alternative explanation of embezzling; they blame it on the weakness,
moral depravity, natural dishonesty, weak moral fibre, etc.,
of the violator. The trouble with explanations of this sort
is that they are always after-the-fact. Such hidden variables
can be said to cause almost any kind of behavior. They usually become evident only after a person has proved that he
is "bad" by stealing from his employer. The notion that an
evil result must have something evil as a cause is a fallacy.

In my own attempt to explain this kind of crime, I spent
about a year at the Illinois State Penitentiary at Joliet inter-
viewing embezzlers. I then moved to California and talked
to some more embezzlers in the California State Institution
for Men at Chino. I was also able to gather a considerable
number of cases from other studies. But I was disturbed
because my sample of embezzlers included very few
bankers; this was because bank embezzlement is a federal
offense and most of my interviews had been conducted in
state prisons. So I spent a summer working in the United
States Penitentiary in Terre Haute, Indiana. From these
interviews I developed a generalization which I think can
be applied to all the embezzlers I talked to. I see no good
reason to believe that it does not apply to all embezzlers,
although I realize that one should not generalize beyond his
data.

What I came up with was the idea that embezzlement
involves three essential kinds of psychological processes:
■ the feeling that a personal financial problem is unshareable;
■ the knowledge of how to solve the problem in secret, by
violating a position of financial trust;

■ the ability to find a formula which describes the act of embezzling in words which do not conflict with the image of oneself as a trusted person.

A man has an *unshareable financial problem* if it appears to him that he cannot turn to ordinary, legitimate sources for funds. To an outsider, the situation may not seem so dire; what matters is the psychological perspective of the potential embezzler. Recently I found an example of this state of mind in a newspaper letter to Ann Landers. The writer was a bookkeeper who had taken $75 from petty cash to pay some long-overdue personal bills. "I could have gone to my boss and received a loan for this amount with no trouble, but I had too much pride. My husband makes a small salary, and I was ashamed to admit we were having a difficult time financially." The writer, who signed herself "Ashamed," was paying the money back, but was terrified that she might succumb to the temptation again.

After I first formulated this unshareable problem notion, I tested it by asking a group of fifty embezzlers about an imaginary financial problem. I asked them to suppose that for some reason their fire insurance policy had lapsed and then, through no fault of their own, there was a short circuit in the wiring, or lightning struck, and their home burned down. The family lost everything they owned in the fire. My question was, "Do you think that in a situation like this you would have been tempted to embezzle to get the money you would need?" Sixty percent of the cases indicated clearly that this situation did not seem to them unshareable, and that therefore they would not embezzle. The reasoning is clear in responses like these:

Case 42. I don't believe I would. I think that in a case like that folks would have sympathized with me and helped me out. There would be outside aid. But in my own case, they didn't know about it and so they couldn't help.

Case 57. Well, I don't doubt that I would if I couldn't borrow the money or something of the sort. There are people or relatives that have money. I've never got along with them, but if it was a necessity like that I would go to them. I'd do anything to give my wife and children what they needed. (He indicated earlier that he had been too proud to go to his relatives for help at the time when he had embezzled.)

The second part of my generalization, the *realization* that the problem could be solved in secret by violating a trust, is a problem in the psychological perception of the opportunity to embezzle. Let me give just one statement, made by an embezzler (and former accountant), about the opportunity and techniques of embezzlement:

In my case, I would have to say that I learned all of it in school and in my ordinary accounting experience. In school they teach you in your advanced years how to detect embezzlements, and you sort of absorb it. . . . It is just like a doctor performing abortions . . . I did not use any techniques which any ordinary accountant in my position could not have used; they are known by all accountants, just like the abortion technique is known by all doctors.

The third process in my generalization, *verbalization*, is the crux of the problem. I am convinced that the *words* that the potential embezzler uses in his conversation with himself are actually the most important elements in the process which gets him into trouble, or keeps him out of trouble. If he sees a possibility for embezzlement, it is because he has defined the relationship between the unshareable problem and an illegal solution in language that lets him look on trust violation as something other than trust violation. If he cannot do this, he does not become an embezzler.

To illustrate, let us suppose a man who is a pillar of the community, a respected, honest employee, a man with a background no more criminal than that of most of us. This man finds himself with an unshareable problem, and an objective opportunity to steal money from his company. The chances are very good that if in that situation I walked up to him and said, "Jack, steal the money from your boss," he would look at me in horror, as if I had suggested that he could solve his problem by going down and sticking a pistol into the face of the local cigar store owner. Honest and trusted men "just don't do such things." However, honest and trusted men do "borrow," and if he tells himself that he is borrowing the money he can continue to believe that he is an honest citizen, even as he is stealing the boss blind. Since he wants to remain an honest citizen, the "borrowing" verbalization becomes the key to his dishonest conduct.

I do not wish to overemphasize the idea of "borrowing." There are many verbalizations used, some of them quite complex. The "borrowing" verbalization is simply an example of a vocabulary that can adjust two contradictory roles—the role of an honest man and the role of a crook. I call the use of such a vocabulary a rationalization, which is different from the way psychoanalysts use the term. Let me give an illustration of rationalization that does *not* involve a dishonest role:

Suppose a Dean who is swamped with work in his university is invited to speak at a seminar of businessmen. He might at first feel he should decline the invitation, on the ground that he doesn't have the time, or he has to get the budget in, or he has to finish writing his book. But then suppose he says to himself, "A Dean should get out of the ivory tower now and then," or "Theoretical knowledge is no good unless it is passed on to practical men." *Now* he can accept the invitation, and does.

Vocabularies of motive are not something invented by embezzlers (or anyone else) on the spur of the moment. Before they can be taken over by an individual, these verbalizations exist as group definitions in which the behavior in question, even crime, is in a sense *appropriate.* There are any number of popular ideologies that sanction crime in our culture: "Honesty is the best policy, but business is business"; "It is all right to steal a loaf of bread when you are starving"; "All people steal when they get in a tight spot"; Once these verbalizations have been assimilated and internalized by individuals, they take a form such as: "I'm only going to use the money temporarily, so I am borrowing, not stealing," or "I have tried to live an honest life but I've had nothing but troubles, so to hell with it."

If my generalization about the psychological elements of embezzling is valid, it should have ramifications for crime prevention. Some change in prevention techniques is clearly necessary, for the embezzlement rate in the United States is on the rise. Increasingly complex business organizations need larger proportions of "trusted employees." Business procedures are becoming so involved that the whole fabric of an enterprise depends more and more upon men who have been given independent control over some segment of the enterprise. At the same time, studies of professional and technical workers indicate that many are dissatisfied with their jobs. These disgruntled employees are potential embezzlers.

It follows from my generalization that embezzling can be

effectively blocked either at the unshareable problem point or at the verbalization point.

■ Trust violation rates might be reduced by eliminating some of the unshareable problems among employees. This means development of company programs so that employees have fewer financial problems and/or feel that they can share their financial problems with their employer. Wherever a company program solves a financial problem, or makes it shareable, embezzlement will not occur.

■ Companies could introduce educational programs that emphasize how trust violators commonly use verbalizations. These programs would make it increasingly difficult for trusted employees to think of themselves as "borrowers" rather than "thieves" when they take the boss's money. It is highly probable that our current practices in this regard actually encourage embezzlement. We tend to emphasize the notion that embezzlers are people who are the victims of "wine, women, and wagering." Because this lore is so popular, a person with an unshareable problem who is not gambling, drinking, or running around with women can easily think of himself as a nonembezzler who is simply "borrowing." What I am proposing is an educational program in which we say over and over again that a person who "pilfers" or "taps the till" or "borrows" or who is guilty of "defalcation," "peculation," or some other nice term is, in fact, a crook. And if the trusted employee rejects the notion of himself as a crook (and as a "respectable" type, he must), he will also reject the possibility of embezzling.

The generalization I have developed here was made to fit only one crime—embezzling. But I suspect that the verbalization section of the generalization will fit other types of respectable crime as well. There is a study of crimes among New England shoe manufacturers that supports this notion. In the eight New England communities studied, there were wide variations in the number of shoe firms violating labor relations laws. In Haverhill, Massachusetts, for example, 7 percent of the shoe firms violated these laws, while in Auburn, Maine, 44 percent violated them. The author, Robert E. Lane, concluded that one of the reasons for the differences among the towns was differences in "attitudes toward the law, the government, and the morality of illegality." Those shoe manufacturers who associated with men whose attitudes favored violation were more likely to break the law; those manufacturers who were isolated from these attitudes were less likely to break the law. This influence on attitudes was evident even in the reading habits of these men; those who had violated the law had immersed themselves in a segment of the daily press so hostile to government that violation of the law seemed quite appropriate to them. Here, even the newspapers were providing verbalizations that made crime "all right." Lane predicted, on the basis of such observations, that managers of companies located in bigger cities, with a cosmopolitan press, diversified social life, and greater tolerance for heterodoxy, would accept legal restrictions on how they conducted their businesses more readily than would small town management. This prediction was borne out; firms located in small towns violated the laws much more frequently than did similar firms located in larger cities. The small town atmosphere provided a rationale to justify this particular crime; (government shouldn't tell a man how to run his business; "that man" in Washington is no good anyway; labor unions are corrupt). The bigger cities did not provide this justification. Another study, by Marshall B. Clinard, analyzed O.P.A. violations during World War II and concluded that businessmen violated the regulations simply because they did not "believe in" them.

The G.E. and Westinghouse officials must have had a formula that made their conspiracy to fix the price of electrical equipment something other than a crime. Perhaps it was a generalized dislike of government regulation of business; perhaps they had convinced themselves that no one really abides by the Sherman Anti-trust Act anyway and that, like the prohibition amendment, it could be transgressed without any stigma of criminality. And surely all the income tax evaders do not see themselves as stealing money from the U.S. Treasury—to them the government may seem so rich that "they'll never miss it" or the intricate tax laws may seem a kind of game that allows an advantage to the shrewd player.

But whether the stakes are high or low, whether the financial game is played by an individual or a conspiring group, an aura of personal respectability does not erase (though it may temporarily obscure), the act of a criminal.

March/April 1965

Abortion Laws
And Their Victims

ALICE S. ROSSI

Millions of Americans have been personally involved in illegal abortions—the women who undergo the operations, their sex partners, and the close confidantes who share the burdens of their experiences, in most cases illegal ones. Despite this widespread personal experience, there has too long been a conspiracy of silence on the subject of abortion.

There are signs that public discussion is increasing—mass media articles, network television programs, popular movies such as "Blue Denim" and "Love with the Proper Stranger," proposals for law reform by various legal and medical bodies. But the focus of public attention is on the most dramatic, though least frequent, situations leading to the desire for abortion—conception through rape or incest, and threats to pregnancies from disease or drugs. Too little attention is paid to the overwhelming number of women

117

who seek abortions, legal or illegal, because they do not want to give birth to an unwelcome or unexpected child.

Also, it is important to note, public discussion comes mainly from professional experts such as gynecologists, obstetricians, public health officials, and specialists in law, demography, family planning, and psychiatry. With rare exception too little is heard from the women directly concerned—those who have undergone the abortion.

Well-publicized abortion cases (such as that of Mrs. Sherry Finkbine who was eventually aborted of a deformed fetus in Europe) involve exposure to German measles during the first trimester of pregnancy or the use of thalidomide early in pregnancy, with its associated high probability of defect in the fetus. But few women who seek abortions have been exposed to German measles or taken thalidomide and hence fear a deformed fetus; few have serious heart or liver conditions that constitute a threat to their life if they carried the pregnancy to term; fewer still have been raped by a stranger or by their own father.

The majority of the women who seek abortions do so because they find themselves with unwelcome or unwanted pregnancies; abortion is a last-resort birth control measure when preventive techniques have failed or have not been used.

It is the situation *of not wanting a child* that covers the main rather than the exceptional abortion situation. But this fact is seldom faced. I believe many people are unwilling to confront this fact because it goes counter to the expectation that women are nurturant, loving creatures who welcome every new possibility of adding a member of the human race. To come to grips with the central motivation that drives women to abortion, *that they do not want the child,* requires admitting that the traditional expectation is a gross oversimplification of the nature of women and the

complex of values which determine their highly individ-
uated response to the prospects of maternity.

When a woman is anxious to conceive a child, there is
nothing to match the joy that attends a confirmation that
she is pregnant, except the actual birth of the baby. If we
take 30 years as the fertility span of a woman, there are
approximately 360 "chances" that she may become pregnant. If she wants and has three children, there will be
some 325 months, or about 90 percent of her potentially
fertile menstrual months, in which she does not have
joyous anticipation of a pregnancy, but rather an under-
current of feelings ranging from vague unease to considerable fear that she may be pregnant. These feelings are not
completely allayed by cognitive confidence in her contraceptive technique. This is true even for women whose contraceptive practices are highly efficacious; for women who
use no contraception, the apprehension is understandably
more acute. Thus, one would think there would be less
resistance to the idea that many women have a dread of
pregnancy and, when they find themselves with an unwanted one, may seek an abortion.

Are America's laws on the subject of abortion in line
with the thinking of its citizens? Before we examine the
varying legal patterns—and both the campaign for reform
and its opponents—let's look at the way the people view
the matter.

Until very recently, there were no organized groups in
the United States supporting abortion reform to match the
very vigorous opposition to such reform. So legislators
had no way of knowing whether the public would greet a
revision in the law negatively or with a response of "it's
about time." Fortunately, there are now indicators available.

A representative sample of 1,484 adult Americans were
asked their views on the conditions under which it should

be possible for a woman to obtain a legal abortion, in a survey conducted by the National Opinion Research Center in December 1965. These adults were asked the following question:

> "Please tell me whether or not you think it should be possible for a pregnant woman to obtain a legal abortion . . ."

They were presented with six varying circumstances, ranging from impairment of the mother's health, to that of a married woman who did not want any more children. The survey results show the majority of the American population support the view that women should be able to obtain a legal abortion under the following circumstances:

- 71 percent if the woman's own health is seriously endangered by the pregnancy.
- 56 percent if she became pregnant as a result of rape.
- 55 percent if there is a strong chance of serious defect in the baby.

When Catholics were compared to Protestant respondents, there was very little religious group difference. Although official Catholic doctrine makes no allowance for abortions in the event of high probability of deformity in the fetus or for pregnancies following sexual assault, close to a majority of Catholic men and women were in favor of legal abortion to cover such situations. Thus, there was no tendency to take an overall doctrinal stand against abortion among Catholics; instead, the range of support they gave varied by situation in precisely the same way that it did among Protestant or Jewish respondents.

Furthermore, the slight tendency for Protestants to be more liberal than Catholics was found to be largely a reflection of differential church attendance, not religious affiliation solely. Frequent church attenders are less likely to take a liberal stand on abortion than those who attend church less frequently *among both groups;* only because Catholics show generally higher church attendance (74 percent) than Protestants do (51 percent) was there any difference in liberal stand on abortion. The data further suggested that education has a "liberalizing" effect on the attitudes of Protestants but not of Catholics—there were no differences in attitudes among poorly educated Protestants and Catholics, but an increasing contrast as educational attainment increased.

Legislators will continue to be exposed to pressure against liberalization of the abortion laws from spokesmen of various religious faiths, but there is a clear support among the electorate from the major religious groups for revision of the existent statutes to cover not merely the life, but also the health, of a pregnant woman or serious risk of deformity in the fetus.

The study also showed that attitudes toward abortion cut across both political orientation and party lines. People with a liberal political orientation who are independent of any political party affiliation, show the most liberal attitudes toward abortion (mean of 51 percent on all six items). But at the next level of liberal views on abortion are Republicans of both liberal (47 percent) and conservative (46 percent) persuasion, and liberal Democrats (42 percent). Those least sympathetic to abortion law reform are conservative Democrats (36 percent) and those who are either politically uncommitted or apolitical.

What the American public clearly does *not* support, however, are abortions in situations which all studies indicate to be the predominant circumstances for women who seek abortions. Support for legal abortions in the remaining three situations is as follows:

- 21 percent if the family has a very low income and cannot afford any more children.
- 18 percent if she is not married and does not want to marry the man.
- 15 percent if she is married and wants no more children.

The analysis showed no differences between Catholics and Protestants on these grounds. What mattered more was education, sex, and general attitude toward sex. Men with at least some college education, for example, are far more likely to approve legal abortions in the case of an unmarried pregnant woman (33 percent) than are women who have had some college training (19 percent) or men (19 percent) and women (9 percent) who have never gone beyond elementary school.

Restrictive attitudes toward premarital sex bear a decided relationship to opposition to legal abortion for every one of the six conditions we specified. Men and women who oppose premarital intercourse between an engaged couple are considerably less likely to approve a legal abortion than those who have a permissive or ambivalent attitude toward premarital intercourse—even where maternal health is endangered or the woman has been sexually assaulted. It is of interest that there are no attitude differences about abortion between men and women among those who hold *restrictive* views toward premarital sex relations; but among those with *permissive* attitudes, men are much more inclined than women to support legal abortions as birth control measures.

Overall then, there is clearly majority support for abortion as a safeguard of maternal health or a prevention of the anguish associated with bearing a deformed child. But any suggestion of abortion as a last-resort means of birth control is firmly rejected by the majority of American adults in the NORC sample. It does not seem to matter what the circumstances are—a poor family for whom an additional child would represent an economic hardship, a single woman who does not wish to marry the man with whom she had sex relations, or a married woman who does not want any more children. The American population approves family planning by means of acceptable contraceptive techniques, but any failure of traditional birth control measures should be followed not by an abortion, but by an acceptance of the pregnancy.

The fact that the last condition—of a married woman who has the number of children she wants—has been the experience of millions of living American women, has not affected public judgment that abortion is "wrong" and should not be legally allowed. The suggestion is strong, therefore, that Americans disapprove of any legitimate institutionalization of a widespread practice if the practice runs counter to the traditional social and religious norms surrounding sex and maternity.

Let us turn now to the law. The perspective of a sociologist and a woman may, it is hoped, contribute to keeping the complex legal and medical considerations from deflecting our attention from the central problem at stake—what society should do for a woman facing an unwanted pregnancy.

State laws vary in the language used and whether the focus is on the mother alone or the mother and the child. In 32 states abortions are unlawful unless they are necessary to "save" or "preserve" the life of the mother. In nine states the preservation of life covers the mother or her child. In only five states and the District of Columbia does the letter of the law go beyond the restriction to saving a life; in Colorado and New Mexico abortions are permitted to preserve the mother's life or prevent "serious bodily injury"; in Alabama, Oregon, and the District of Columbia, the law exempts abortions designed to preserve the life or "health" of the mother. Only in Maryland is the legal phrasing more general: the state law exempts abortions which would "secure the safety of the mother."

These statutes come under the criminal code. The goal of abortion reform groups has been concentrated on seeking a change in this penal code. Revision proposals are most frequently based on the Model Penal Code recommended by the American Law Institute in 1959. The clauses relevant to abortion extend exemption from criminal prosecution to cases in which the continuance of the pregnancy involves "substantial risk that mother or child will suffer grave and irremediable impairment of physical or mental health" or where the pregnancy "resulted from forcible rape." Thus, if there is a high probability of defect in the fetus or serious physical or psychological impairment of the mother should she carry the fetus to term, and if the presence of these circumstances is certified by at least two physicians, then a legal abortion will be possible under this revised code, and the doctors involved have a justifiable affirmative defense.

It is this revised penal code clause which has received rather widespread endorsement. Variations of it have been reviewed and hearings held in the legislatures of several states—Illinois, Minnesota, New Hampshire, California, and New York. In no case has reform yet succeeded. So too, the recommendation of the Committee on Human Reproduction of the AMA favoring law reform was turned down by the House of Delegates of the AMA, which referred the problem back to the Board of Trustees with a recommendation that the problem be explored "in depth with other interested groups."

Where illegal abortion is concerned, the estimated range of operations is from 250,000 to somewhat over 1,000,000 per year in the United States. We are on somewhat firmer ground in gauging the incidence of legal abortions conducted in hospital settings, particularly when they are based on statistics from municipalities in which such abortions are required to be justified and recorded. The most recent estimate for the United States is somewhere between 8,000 and 10,000.

Yet, to many people opposed to law reform this is not a "significant" problem because there is no agreement on exactly how extensive the incidence of illegal abortion is. Further, many persons refuse to believe even the lower limit of the estimated range, on the grounds that they personally know of no woman who has had an illegal abortion.

Also, they say, there is no need to change the law because abortion is declining, as contraceptive practices become more widespread and more effective.

Is the incidence rate a proper basis for deciding whether this is a major social problem or not? Medical researchers do not avoid attempts to find a cure for a rare disease because the chances are it will cripple or kill only 10,000 people a year. We do not consider unemployment a minor social problem because more than 90 percent of the labor force is employed. We do not rest content with educational attainment of American youth because the majority now complete a high school education.

The same reasoning should apply to the abortion problem. Those who argue with the incidence estimates, or resist change in our abortion laws on the grounds that it is not an extensive social problem, are either deluding us or themselves as to what is really at the heart of their disclaimers: they do not wish to see any liberalization of abortion laws because they are opposed to abortion per se; or they have little or no empathy for the women who want to obtain one; or they consciously or unconsciously believe the psychologically punishing and medically and legally risky experience of securing an illegal abortion is deserved —it is a *punishment* for becoming pregnant if you are poor or unmarried or already have a large family.

There is enormous variation from hospital to hospital, city to city, one physician to another in the ratio of therapeutic abortions to deliveries. One doctor may perform one abortion to every four or five deliveries, while another performs one abortion to every 2,000 deliveries. A private hospital with financially well-off patients, may perform one legal abortion in every 36 deliveries, while another hospital, one which treats clinic patients, has a record of no legal abortions in 24,417 deliveries.

The grounds justifying legal therapeutic abortions have changed over the years. Psychological justification has increased as strictly medical considerations of physical health have declined. Doctors have shown a gradual broadening of their conception of "health" to include many non-physical factors in the woman's condition, a reflection of the slow penetration of psychoanalytic theory into medical training and medical thinking. The decline in abortions for medical reasons is also a reflection of medical progress: as tuberculosis declined in the population at large, so it declined as justification for legal abortions. As knowledge is acquired about the effect of radiation, rubella, or thalidomide upon the probability of defect in the fetus, new grounds for legal abortion enter the picture.

Following the model of the Scandinavian countries, there has been a marked trend in the United States since the 1950's toward the establishment of hospital abortion boards to review potential cases of abortion. Studies have shown that hospitals following this committee device have lower therapeutic abortion rates than hospitals without such committees; the establishment of the committees can be interpreted as a self-protecting response on the part of the medical profession against the trend toward an increasing number of legal abortions for psychological reasons.

The effect of liberalization of abortion laws upon subsequent patterns of live births and abortion rates can be gleaned by analysis of data from other countries. One pattern is clear: the birth rate declines more rapidly following such abortion liberalization than by any comparable measure such as contraceptive campaigns. This is nowhere more dramatically shown than in Japan since the passage of the Eugenic Protection Law in 1948. This act comes closer to abortion-on-demand than any abortion legislation anywhere in the world. The success of this policy in halting the skyrocketing population increase in Japan can be seen by comparing the rate of live births and of legal abortions in the year following the passage of the act, 1949, and comparable rates for 1962: the rate of live births per 1,000 population declined from 33.2 in 1949 to 17.0 in 1962, while the rate of legal abortions per 1,000 population increased from 3.0 to 10.4. This rapid increase in abortions during the 1950's was due mainly to older women aborting pregnancies after they already had a number of children.

Much the same story applies to countries in Eastern Europe. In Hungary, for example, which introduced interruption of pregnancy "on-request" in 1956, the number of legal abortions increased rapidly; by 1961 abortions exceeded the number of live births by more than one-fifth. The fact that the birth rate declined in East European countries which have liberalized abortion laws, but did *not* decline in the two countries which did not legalize abortion

(Albania and East Germany) is strong evidence that the legalization of abortion depressed the birth rate.

It may be, incidentally, that the most dramatic birth rate reduction, in countries whose population is growing at alarming rates, would result from a two-part program: liberalization of abortion laws which women will respond to (pregnancy being primarily "women's concern"), and contraceptive campaigns aimed at the men (sex being "men's concern").

What is known about the pattern of *illegal abortion* cases is necessarily on less confident grounds:

■ Roughly one in five of the women in the Kinsey study who were ever married reported induced abortions. While this sample is not completely representative of the American population, somewhat greater confidence can be placed in the Kinsey picture of subgroup variations in the proportion reporting induced abortions. They found that induced abortions increase with the number of pregnancies terminated in marriage, testimony to the fact that women resort to abortion for pregnancies which occur after they have reached the family size they desire. The relationship shown by age and education is similarly interesting for the social pattern it suggests: among poorly educated women, the highest rate of induced abortion is among the older women; among well-educated women, the highest rate is among the younger women. What this suggests is that poorly educated women who become pregnant, either have illegitimate children (particularly if they are Negro), or marry and have the first child within wedlock, and abort their later pregnancies. Well-educated women abort their premarital pregnancies, marry later and use more reliable contraceptive techniques with more cooperative husbands to control their family size.

■ The abortion rate, like the fertility rate, is responsive

to the economic cycle in the society. By comparing the rate of reported induced abortions with the age when they were performed, Paul Gebhard shows that abortions were probably greater during the depression and declined in the 1940's and 1950's.

The official Catholic position on abortion has held simply that nothing may be done which would involve any direct killing of the fetus. The only exception is the application of the Catholic rule of "double effect" or "indirect killing." Catholic obstetricians may remove an ectopic pregnancy or a cancerous pregnant uterus because these operations have the primary purpose of saving the life of the mother, not the killing of the fetus, which is secondary.

Whatever the position of the church, the actual behavior of Catholics is quite another matter. Countries with predominantly Roman Catholic populations actually show high abortion rates, as they do of illegitimacy. In a recent survey of Roman Catholic Chile, for example, 27 percent of the women reported they had had induced abortions. In Roman Catholic France, the annual number of abortions equals the annual number of live births.

A religious group is free to characterize abortion as a sin if it sees fit to do so and to punish its members for this by some appropriate ecclesiastical censure if it wishes. The rest of the society should, however, enjoy the right to control their own reproductive lives in accordance with their conception of morality and human dignity.

Apart from the fine points of theology and ethical consideration, there is a quality of sentimentality about the defense of the right of the fetus to be born that strikes at least this feminine ear as alien to the ways and the feelings of women one has known or studied. I have never heard a woman wax sentimental about 300 or so ova which are never fertilized, nor have I heard remorse expressed for a two-month-old fetus that is spontaneously aborted. It is not the loss of a particular fetus a woman grieves over, but the loss of her potential maternity and potential baby. In a similar way, despite all claims to the contrary, there is no evidence that women who have had induced abortions are typically stricken with guilt and remorse as an aftermath. The few cases of women who do feel such regret must be weighed against the human price in bitterness, economic hardship, and psychological stress that is paid by the woman, her family, and the unwanted child if she does *not* obtain an abortion.

It would appear to be a matter of time and the continued and extended efforts of men and women who work for abortion reform, until American law will undergo some degree of liberalization. It is still an open question, however, how widespread the trend will be in various states to remove abortion from coverage by the criminal law (no other medical procedure is regulated by criminal law) and to place it under either civil statutes bearing on the licensing of physicians, or, more positively, statutes bearing on the regulation of hospitals. Either of these latter two changes would clearly and firmly shift responsibility to the medical profession.

But if we rest content with goals limited to the penal code revision that is most likely to be passed, we shall scarcely have helped many women in the United States. Nor will such passage of a revised code be followed by any significant increase in legal abortions and decrease in illegal abortions, since the law will not cover most of the women who now have abortions illegally. Married women who do not want to have a third or fourth child (or an unmarried woman who does not want to marry the man by whom she has conceived, or who does not want to marry her) will still be faced with a cruel choice between deceitful lying in order to get a legal abortion, or being honest about her motivation and seeking an illegal one.

Let us take, as an example, the plight of an unmarried woman who becomes pregnant. What alternatives does our society offer her, and what is the consequence for the woman and for the society?

■ *Marry the man by whom she conceived.* The price?— a high-risk marriage. There is no period for the mutual exploration of each other and adjustment to marriage itself, but a double task of adjusting to pregnancy and anticipated maternity while also adjusting to spouse, sex, and obligations of home maintenance. The outcome—a high probability of divorce and separation, a couple cheated of the joy and adventure and independence of the pre-parenthood stage of marriage, more children reared in fatherless homes, and strained relations between the woman and her parents, who are so often firmly insistent on the daughter's marriage as the solution to her pregnancy out of wedlock.

■ *Go through with the pregnancy and put the child up for adoption.* There are few writers in the literature on abortion who have stressed what many women in this situation feel deeply—the cruelty and sadism that is involved when her doctor, parents, minister, lawyer, or social worker suggest that she carry the child to term and then hand it over, never to see it again, to someone else to raise. It is a heartless recommendation, and psychiatrists inform us it creates far more difficult and extensive therapeutic problems than with patients who have an abortion early in pregnancy.

■ *Have the child illegitimately and rear it herself.* The price? Ask those engaged currently in trying to break the vicious cycle of poverty in the lower working class of our large cities: women with double responsibility as breadwinner and mother working at jobs for which they do not receive equal pay for equal work; encounters with men who do not want to assume responsibility for another man's child; children who often suffer from neglect to outright maternal rejection.

■ *Have an abortion*—if she has the good fortune to contact a physician courageous enough to recommend her for a legal abortion, or refer her to another physician for an illegal abortion.

To withhold the possibility of a safe and socially acceptable abortion for unmarried women is to start the chain of illegitimacy and despair that will continue to keep poverty, crime, and poor mental health high on the list of pressing social problems in the United States. Finally, it is expecting entirely too much of human frailty and the complex motivations underlying human sexual behavior to think abortions will no longer be necessary when contraceptive techniques are perfected and universally used. One has only to observe carefully the adaptive role the woman plays in sex in Mirra Komarovsky's *Blue Collar Marriage* or Lee Rainwater's *Workingman's Wife* and *And the Poor Get Children* to understand some of the limitations upon the consistent use of contraceptives by large numbers of American women. Furthermore, not all women can take the pill, nor be fitted with a ring, and pregnancies even occur in both types of birth control.

Social approval is extended to the woman who plans her family size and child spacing well by using the best contraceptive technique available and suitable for her, but if these measures fail, the only alternative is acceptance of pregnancy she does not want, or the unsafe and traumatic experience of an illegal abortion. Any woman, whether married or not, should be able to secure a safe abortion, upon her own request, at a reasonable fee, in a licensed hospital by a licensed and competent physician.

September 1966

Assassination
In the Middle East

CARL LEIDEN

The Middle East is a suitable area to study assassinations. Not only have many assassinations of various types occurred there but many different political systems coexist within the area. The study of assassination, however, and especially of assassination in the Middle East, raises a number of problems. Perhaps the most urgent is the need to define the term. Appropriately enough, the word "assassin" is of Arabic origin. It derives from the Arabic *hashīshiyyīn,* meaning "those who use hashish," and refers to one of the Shiite Ismaili sects in the Syria of the eleventh century. For a time, this sect made political advances by murdering its opponents, the killers allegedly obtaining their courage by the use of hashish.

For our purposes, we must differentiate between assassination and other acts of violence, notably murder. An old synonym for assassination, indeed, was "political murder." Yet assassination is *not* merely murder. In the old *En-*

cyclopedia of the Social Sciences, Max Lerner states that
assassination "refers to the killing of a person in public
life from a political motive and without legal process." It
is the political aspect that distinguishes assassination from
murder. The victim need not be a political *leader,* but such
an assassination has a greater systemic impact and is con-
sequently of greater interest. In general, assassination seems
to refer to those killings or murders, largely directed
against individuals in public life, motivated by political
rather than by personal relationships.

I think it would be useful to view assassination as a
function of certain variables. And I would suggest that the
greater the prominence of the victim, the more the motive
was impersonal (no unfaithful wife), the greater the impact upon the public, and the more the victim was unrelated
to the slayer, the more likely a killing is to be an assassination.

Less urgent is the need for a study of the rationaliza-
tions of assassination in the Middle East. Although assassination has always characterized Muslim history—three of
the first four caliphs were assassinated—there has never
been much theoretical justification for it. Other questions
whose answers should be sought are: What connections
exist between assassination and religious extremism or nationalism? In what stages of political or economic development is assassination more likely? Does assassination feed
upon itself with the likelihood of more assassination pro-
portional to the intensity of assassination in any particular
area?

It is also important to separate various types of assassinations in terms of their political significance. Some assassinations bring about no measurable changes in political systems. Example: the assassination of the Lebanese political
leader, Riad al-Solh, in Amman in 1951. And one must

judge significance in terms of relativity. In 1954, for example, an attempt was made on the life of Egypt's President Gamal Abdel Nasser. Had it succeeded, the entire history of the Middle East would have been altered. Yet his death then would have been far less significant than his death by assassination *in 1967*. Ultimately it may be necessary to characterize an assassination's significance as a function of variables that are peculiar to some particular political system.

How many assassinations must a society endure before we can say that it is assassination-prone? I myself doubt that "sheer quantity" means much. What is important is which leaders are assassinated. As for the question of how many assassinations a political system can bear before it breaks down, the Middle Eastern experience suggests that every political system—except perhaps the now defunct South Arabia Federation—shows a remarkable ability to absorb assassinations.

Is assassination an index of other, more serious, political violence? Does it presage revolution? At this time, research on the Middle East permits only tentative answers. Thus, many assassinations in the Middle East are simply by-products of other activities, notably coups d'états. Such assassinations may have little significance in and of themselves. On the other hand, there are assassinations that serve as safety valves, and instead of precipitating further violence tend to reduce its likelihood.

Finally, it would seem that assassinations are often significant to a political system when either of these conditions holds true:

1) The political system is organized so as to place massive authority in a few hands. (This is certainly true of the Middle East. Recall Egypt's explanation for her military failure in 1967: Her high command was aloft, and there-

fore isolated, during the early Israeli air strikes.)

2) When the personal influence of certain individuals has become intense and deep-rooted. (This is also certainly true of the Middle East. Nowhere else is there more dependence upon personal leadership, personal following, and personal political attachment.)

It is not that when one or the other of these conditions obtains, assassination is more likely, but rather that when assassinations occur, they are likely to have greater political impact.

As for the motives behind an assassination, an examination of a large number of assassinations in the Middle East suggests the typology that follows, a typology that may not be applicable everywhere. (In addition, one assassination may have more than one motive.) Assassination occurs because of:

- personal or family grievances (Note the marginal nature of such assassination.)
- the desire for political revenge
- the symbolic benefits to be derived from the death of the victim
- the practical need for removal
- the need for unofficial executions
- the need for a scapegoat

A good example of personal revenge as a motive was the assassination of Nadir Shah of Afghanistan on Nov. 8, 1933, by a 17-year-old student, Mohammed Kaleq, whose father by adoption, General Ghulam Nabi Charkhi, had been executed by the Shah almost exactly a year before. There was little significance to this assassination. The Shah's son, Zahir Shah, became the ruler; his uncles gave the government political direction. The current Afghan constitution calls Nadir Shah "The Martyr," but despite such commendations and despite the genuinely fine qualities that the Shah possessed, he has been little remembered. The Middle East abounds in such assassinations for personal or family grievances, but most of these killings were of limited importance.

The desire for political revenge is another common cause of assassinations, and the consequences in these cases are usually major. The murder of King Abdullah Ibn Hussein of Jordan is the classic example.

In 1951, the Arab world was still seething from its failure to destroy the newly established state of Israel. Discontent had already manifested itself in a series of military coups in Syria, and was to result in a coup in Egypt in 1952.

On July 20, 1951, when Abdullah entered the mosque of al-Aqsa in Jerusalem, he was shot by an adherent of Haj Amin al-Husseini, the old Mufti of Jerusalem, and a long time political foe of Abdullah.

Abdullah's Arab Legion had been the only Arab military force that had enjoyed much success against the Israelis but Abdullah himself had proved the most willing to come to a modus vivendi with the Israelis. His slaying seems to have been political revenge against the one Arab who symbolized moderation in his approaches to Israel. The act itself had immediate implications for Jordan and for the remainder of the Arab world. Abdullah was strongly supported by the British, was closely tied to the ruling family of Iraq, and was the great moderate of Arab politics.

The third motive—the desire for symbolic benefits—applies when a public leader is slain for no direct reason whatsoever, but his killing symbolizes the "evil" of those he represents, the strength of the assassin's group, or simply the importance of the victim and his position. The Middle East furnishes a number of examples, and two of the most interesting involve the Israelis.

In November 1944 in Cairo, two members of the Israeli terrorist organization, the Stern gang—Eliahu Bet Zouri, 22, and Eliahu Hakim, 17—shot and killed Lord Moyne, British Minister of State in the Middle East. The assassins apparently believed that by their act they could hasten the departure of the British from Palestine and hasten the establishment of Israel. Their deed was later eulogized and commemorated by Gerold Frank—in *The Deed,* 1963— who argues that, "no person, no time, no place, could have been chosen more likely to result in embarrassment to the British. . . . But there is no doubt that the deed was one of the great irritations, the great harassments, which so annoyed and confused and bedeviled the British that ultimately they gave the problem over to the United Nations— and thus opened the door to the partition of Palestine and the first Jewish State in two thousand years." The event actually was hardly so significant.

More important was the assassination of Count Folke Bernadotte, the United Nations mediator in Palestine. On Sept. 17, 1948, Bernadotte was killed by a submachine-gun blast from a man whose associates were dressed in Israeli army uniforms. Members of the Stern gang publicly claimed credit for the assassination. Revenge was not involved, nor was Bernadotte's removal essential. But his death symbolized that no halfway measures would be tolerated by extremist Israelis in the negotiations going on with respect to the Arab frontiers and refugees. The assassination cast a pall over the area and its issues, and undoubtedly a certain "success" was obtained by the act.

A fourth motive is the practical need for removal—the physical presence of the victim is inimical to the plans of the assassin or of his group. It is one of the more common motives for assassination in the Middle East, and such killings can have enormous significance. Example: the removal of Nokrashy Pasha, the Prime Minister of Egypt, in 1948.

Nokrashy became Prime Minister in 1945, and in the years that followed—years that saw the Israeli-Arab war in Palestine—he took steps to control the terrorist Muslim Brotherhood. In December 1948, Nokrashy was shot and killed—by a member of the Brotherhood. There were many possible reasons for the assassination, but the most persuasive is that Nokrashy was simply an impediment, and there were pragmatic benefits if he could be gotten out of the way. Nokrashy's presence was undermining the ambitions of the Brotherhood's leaders, and by his death they hoped to see a new government that would be more compliant with their demands. The assassination itself was a disastrous failure so far as reaching the goals of the Brotherhood was concerned, but the failure itself had great importance.

Indeed, assassination as a deliberate national policy has even been undertaken in the Middle East. Clandestine radio stations broadcast appeals to the citizenry of other states to assassinate their rulers. In 1962, Cairo radio broadcast this message to the Iraqis: "Freemen, heroes, makers of the 14 July revolution, fate has sent you a clown. It has sent you Abdel Karim Qasim, who sees nothing in Iraq but himself. . . . You destroyed the palaces of Faysal and Abd al-Ilah and dragged their bodies in the streets. You can do the same thing to this clown. So march on the Defense Ministry and destroy Qasim."

A variant of the practical need for removal is the fifth motive—the need for unofficial executions. Here, a government conspires in the assassination, usually because the country lacks a legal death penalty or because the political climate will not permit a successful trial of the victim. Example: the assassination of Sheikh Hassan el-Banna, the head of the Brotherhood that had taken Nokrashy's life.

Banna was not only the leader of the Brotherhood at the time of Nokrashy's death, but its founder. A man of ability and energy, and possessed with charisma as well, Banna had incredible ambitions—politically to run Egypt, religiously to become caliph. His removal of Nokrashy brought to power Ibrahim Abdul Hadi Pasha, who was determined to destroy the Brotherhood. Equally important, King Farouk became frightened of the open, callous destructiveness of the Brotherhood.

It is not likely that we shall ever have all the facts about what happened, but trustworthy authorities suggest the following:

Badly frightened by the wave of terrorism brought about by the Brotherhood, the king and his government felt compelled to move against Banna himself. It would have been utterly impossible in the atmosphere of winter 1948 to try Banna legally for conspiracy in the death of Nokrashy. The only alternative seemed direct action. In February 1949, Banna was publicly shot and killed in Cairo by agents of the (secret) police. Although "investigated," the crime was never "cleared up."

In this case, assassination was resorted to by a government too weak or too frightened to use its legal measures of repression. (An excellent historical example of this sort of thing was the many-splendored politics of Catherine de Medici in sixteenth-century France.)

A final motive: scapegoat-substitution. In other words, a victim is chosen in order to divert guilt for other sins from the assassin's group to the victim—with the victim no longer being around, or having the power, to defend himself. Should the Egyptian army kill Nasser in response to the humiliation it must bear for its defeat at the hands of the Israelis, the assassination might well be a clear example of scapegoat-substitution. An actual example: the death of General Bakr Sidqi in 1937, which gave Iraqi politicians and generals an opportunity to load him with guilt and opprobrium for crimes they themselves were blamed with.

In October 1936, Sidqi overthrew the civilian government of Iraq and propped up a new government for nearly a year. Sidqi retained his command over the army, but did not accept ministerial rank. The year was not an easy one in Iraq. Civilian leaders were divided over questions of reform. Sidqi's inchoate ambitions led to civilian confusions and military uncertainties. On August 11, 1937, while Sidqi was resting at the Mosul airport, a soldier—acting on behalf of a well-planned conspiracy—fired two shots at the general, killing him instantly.

Although the general had many friends in the army and in the government, the army itself frustrated attempts to uncover and punish the conspirators. A dead General Sidqi, even buried as he was with full military honors, could be loaded with all the guilts and failings of the army and the regime.

It seems likely that research in assassination in the Middle East will prove to be a most fruitful endeavor. Political systems in change, those undergoing stress, are precisely those most likely to exhibit their basic structures to public view. Therefore, if assassinations do have effects on a political system, and if we can discover what these effects are, we will also have learned something important about the structure of that system.

May 1969

FURTHER READING SUGGESTED BY THE AUTHOR:

Against the Tyrant by Oscar Jászi and John D. Lewis (Glencoe, Ill.: The Free Press, 1957) contains a long section on the concept of tyrannicide in Western philosophy and a pragmatic section on the typology of assassination.

The Assassins by Bernard Lewis (New York: Basic Books, 1968)
is not only an excellent book on the origins of the word "assassin"
and of the religious group called the Assassins, but also
contains general commentary on assassination.

Kennedy's Death: Myths and Realities

IRVING LOUIS HOROWITZ

"What has violence ever accomplished? What has it ever created? No martyr's cause has ever been stilled by his assassin's bullet. . . . Whenever we tear at the fabric of life which another man has painfully and clumsily woven for himself and his children, the whole nation is degraded. . . . There is another kind of violence, slower but just as deadly, destructive as the shot or the bomb in the night. This is the violence of institutions; indifference and inaction and slow decay. This is the violence that afflicts the poor, that poisons relations between men because their skin has different colors. . . . But we can perhaps remember—even if only for a time—that those who live with us are our brothers, that they share with us the same short movement of life, that they seek—as we do—nothing but the chance to live out their lives in purpose and happiness, winning what satisfaction and fulfillment they can."

Robert F. Kennedy in Cleveland, Ohio, on April 5, 1968
the day following the assassination of Martin Luther King.

143

These reflections upon the murder of Senator Robert F. Kennedy are an effort to match the reality of regicide with the necessity for political mobilization. In times of crisis, Americans react with a sense of guilt by acclamation, and this guilt prompts us to respond to political assassination with moral outrage, not with action. The answer to terror, however, is not tears, but—in this case—the immediate restatement of the principles of legitimation upon which this nation is either to survive or to perish.

The myths already circulated by major political figures about the assassination of Senator Kennedy can be categorized into five types. The significance of the assassination compels an attempt to respond to these myths, not in the spirit of belligerence, but in an attempt to move us all beyond the state of shock.

FIRST MYTH: *Assassination has become a contagious and infectious American style.*

REALITY: While it is true that major political figures are periodically subjected to assassination attempts, these attempts are usually restricted to the top leadership, and this has been constant throughout the century. Hardly a President has not had attempts on his life. More significantly, the murder of Senator Kennedy is only distantly related to earlier native efforts. When Sirhan Bishara Sirhan was captured, he said: "I did it for my country. I love my country." But this country turned out to be Jordan, not the United States. In his mind, apparently, there was a fevered, imaginary relationship between an adolescent experience of his, and Kennedy's acceptance of the principle of foreign aid for Israel. What is involved, therefore, is a *political* pathology more than a *psycho*pathology. And although this prosaic fact may counter the demands of oracles and pundits for greater social controls, it shows the need to frame a response relevant to the role of prevalent ideologies of Middle East nationalism. Although the Jordanian ambassador may sincerely repudiate this assassination, the fact remains that the ideology promoting such an attempt remains intact. The blunt truth is that assassination is far more common in Middle East antipolitics than in United States politics.

SECOND MYTH: *The degree of violence has increased as the propensity to change has accelerated.*

REALITY: The propensity to violence is, unfortunately, far more constant than current rhetoric would have it. At least there is as much evidence that accelerated social change directs aggressive impulses into acceptable frameworks as there is that "social order" permits a greater degree of social cohesiveness. What *is* new has little to do with matters relating to "human nature," whatever that amorphous beast may turn out to be. Rather, the novel elements are, first, the incredibly easy access to weaponry of all sorts for all kinds of people; and the extent to which nonentities can become part of universal history by an act of regicide—an act linked to the publicity provided for an event. Easy access to weapons plus total network coverage equals instant history. With weapons, impulsivities formerly bottled up or redirected along constructive lines can be quickly ventilated. Impulse is even given ideological support: One wing of the New Politics perceives of the role of the individual or the conspiratorial group in terms of tearing up established political continuities.

THIRD MYTH: *Madmen and criminal elements will always be able to avail themselves of weapons, and therefore any legislation against gun-toting penalizes only the innocent interested in self-protection.*

REALITY: Admittedly, laws against gun purchasers, like laws against discrimination, will not result in the elimination of crime, any more than civil rights legislation does away with racism. But there is no evidence that gun-toting is a basic human appetite. More important, laws would make purchases more difficult and registration-tightening would make tracking out ownership easier. Perhaps at the heart of the problem is not the lobbying of the National Rifle Association, but the fears of the police that laws against free distribution of weapons would eventually affect police departments—since the militarization of the police would also have to be curbed if any genuine enforcement is to be made possible. In short, legislation on gun registration is needed to develop the "Londonization" of the police, no less than the pacification of the civilian population.

FOURTH MYTH: *Since there is no evidence that there is a conspiracy in most political assassinations, as in the murder of Robert Kennedy, individual responsibility should be assigned; and when captured, the guilty person should be treated as demented or deranged.*

REALITY: There are several fallacies in this line of reasoning. A premature dismissal of possible conspiracies, at least as a starting point in explaining political murder, is absurd. Conspiracies are empirical events. One can have a conspiracy, in fact, without a theory of conspiracy to guide the search for the source of a crime. Further, conspiracies —when they do take place—are extremely difficult to detect or uncover. But again, this is a problem of empirics, not of assumptions. The idea that an assassination is an idiosyncratic matter, while perhaps reassuring to the general populace, returns the problem of regicide to the field of personal pathology. In a thoroughly unconvincing way, it disposes of fanaticism that is linked to reinforced nationalist claims or ethnic affiliations. By broadening the interpretation of conspiracy, and by treating this attempt as having precisely such a collective source, the assassination of Senator Kennedy permits renewed efforts to obtain a Middle

East settlement—just as the assassination of Martin Luther King clearly triggered settlements of labor disputes in Memphis and led the way for a more positive Congressional response to the Washington Poor Peoples' March. There is a pragmatic advantage in making the fewest possible assumptions about assassination attempts, but when assumptions are made, there is little justification and less payoff in choosing individual over collective modalities of explanation.

FIFTH MYTH: *The assassination attempts on men of stature, such as Senator Kennedy, drastically affect the course of history.*

REALITY: Let it be said that this myth is hard to combat or overcome directly. It is always difficult to assess the importance of an individual to the future course of historic events. Such an assessment entails an estimate of the degree to which individuals in politics are autonomous, or at least free to maneuver the ship of state as they wish. It is quite as difficult to judge how new events might change old leaders, no less than how old leaders might shape new events. But there is no need to become excessively metaphysical in such discussion. Attention might simply be drawn to the fact that the same social and political problems exist in 1968 that existed at the time of President John F. Kennedy's assassination in 1963. The war in Vietnam remains. Racial violence is increasing. On the other side, the thawing of the Cold War between the United States and the Soviet Union has continued at roughly the same pace under President Johnson. This is not to deny that changes in substance as well as style are brought about by an assassination; it is to say that problems of social structure and historical determination remain intact. However important the role of leadership in political organization may be, the role of total populations is, after all, far greater and more pervasive. Politics in America is still a game of large numbers. No political assassination can alter that fact without destroying American democracy. As there is guilt, so too there is guilt alleviation. And the basic form this has taken under the Johnson administration has been the commission. We get riot commissions in place of urban renewal; crime commissions instead of full employment; and now a commission to investigate "violence in American life" in place of full political participation. It might be said that the candidacy of Robert F. Kennedy was dedicated to the overthrow of the bureaucratization and Washington-centered nature of current administration efforts. By a quirk of events, his death has led to a new commission—to the very phenomenon Kennedy found such an abomination. Sentimentality and brutality are first cousins—which is why they appear to coalesce so well in the present administrative "style."

The formation of a commission on violence only makes more remote a resolution of the political dilemmas besetting the American nation. These dilemmas have been eloquently spoken of in the Democratic primaries. In the remarkable showings of both Kennedy and McCarthy, it is no exaggeration to say that the vote against the war in Vietnam and against the mishandling of the present urban crisis indicate a full appreciation on the part of the electorate of both the nature of and the constraints upon violence. The formation of a commission can only have the effect of psychologizing and blunting the political nature of violence.

Throughout the California primaries it was clear that Kennedy's strength and survival depended upon a large outpouring of poor people and their spokesmen. Black Americans, Mexican-Americans, and the other ethnic and religious minorities that comprise a large segment of the

California population demonstrated by their vote that Kennedy's tactic was also a principle. An estimated 80 percent of the Negro voters and 85 percent of the Mexican-American voters cast their ballots for Kennedy. Less than one week later, on Friday, June 7, at Saint Patrick's Cathedral in New York, citizens of the same background—indeed, it was only that the Puerto Ricans displaced the Mexican-Americans with their presence—also cast their ballots symbolically. The remarkable gathering of hundreds of thousands of people through the night was more than a celebration of mystical martyrdom. Every man, woman, and child who placed his or her hand on the casket was registering a vote, a vote denied to them by the assassination.

Such a society has a great reservoir of political health and sophistication. That it is precisely this sector of society that must suffer the consequences of this latest political murder is made terrible by the knowledge that in this way the poor have been effectively disenfranchised. The assassination creates a situation of political desocialization at the very moment when Kennedy for the minorities and McCarthy for the students and other disaffected citizens were revitalizing the very mainsprings of political socialization. In this sense the appointment of a commission on violence is a fruitless as well as a thankless task, since the very act of depoliticalization is the source of further violence. The assassination of Robert Kennedy was an act of terrorism. To convert it into the basis for a feeling of collective guilt for increased violence is to ignore a basic fact of our times not only in the United States but throughout the world. Violence can and often is a political act, the first mature step beyond egotistic resolution of social problems. Terrorism is the very opposite and negation of violence, since it frustrates and makes impossible the fruits of these very activities.

In his own way, Kennedy not only supported but drew sustenance from the "participatory democracy" advocates. Leaders of social-protest movements, new agrarian unions, and community racial and ethnic societies formed an urban backbone for Kennedy with which to take on the "party regulars." There is no doubt that he was hardly the favorite politician of Washington insiders. His audacious attempt to use the mass media to break the stranglehold of locked-in party organization was not to be dismissed lightly. The attacks on the Kennedy wealth were in fact not a resentment of the economic "oligarchical" tendencies of this wealth, but a resentment of the populist goals to which this wealth was placed. The Kennedy "coalition" of urban poor, ethnic and racial minorities, and a section of college and university personnel made the Democratic Party the natural home for these people. The assassination has changed the alignments but not the needs. In this sense, populism must readjust its vision of the politicians— and estimate the short-run and long-run damage occasioned by Kennedy's death, and realize that organizational rather than charismatic channels may now be required.

Social scientists will feel a special loss, too, for Kennedy made use of social-science personnel and findings in areas extending from Latin American aid programs to urban rehabilitation and renewal. As he wrote to me on June 3, "I have always believed that it is crucial to be assisted by social scientists in their particular fields in forming domestic and foreign policy."

The urgency of the age demands a movement, not a monument; confrontation, not conformity. The time for demonstrations of public sorrow passes quickly—despite the monstrous fact that within two months our nation has lost two of its staunchest fighters against current policies guiding the war in Vietnam and the war in the ghettos at home. It is now time to translate sentiments into politics. When all participate equally, the loss of a leader such as Robert F. Kennedy will be seen as the brutal price that men often pay in the struggle for a democratic society.

July/August 1968

Why Kennedy Was Killed

HERBERT J. GANS

The murder of Robert F. Kennedy is closely related to that of Martin Luther King, John F. Kennedy, Medgar Evers, the three civil-rights workers who died in Philadelphia, Miss., and the many anonymous victims of Southern racists. I believe that all of the murders were carried out to impede the process of social change now going on in America.

Most of these men became martyrs in and for the advancement of civil rights, but the process of social change to which I refer goes far beyond this noble cause. It is partly a demand for more *equality,* economic, social, racial, and political by those now unequal, but also for more *democracy,* for greater participation in the decisions of the bureaucracies and corporate bodies that now govern much of our daily life.

Although the people who presently demand more equality come mainly from the ghetto, and those who press for more democracy are mostly college students, I am convinced that, in the future, similar demands will come from many other groups in American society—for example, from white-collar and blue-collar workers employed by autocratically-run institutions, be these corporations, government offices, newspapers, or churches, and from people of all classes living under autocratic political organizations.

Robert Kennedy, like most of the other victims of assassins, was a leader in this process. Although in some ways he remained loyal to the traditional political Establishment, I believe he saw the widespread demand for more equality and democracy—and not just from poor blacks—and was grappling with how it could be achieved in an orderly fashion. It is true, of course, that R.F.K. was shot by a Jordanian who was angered by his pro-Israel stand, but I believe the reason he killed Kennedy rather than other pro-Israel political leaders was Kennedy's fervent enthusiasm for basic change in American politics and policies that went far beyond the rhetorical enthusiasm of most liberal politicians.

Today we grieve for Robert Kennedy, but tomorrow we must start to ask why social change in American is so often accompanied by political violence, and seemingly more so than in other Western societies. The popular media have begun to argue that ours is a sick society, covered by a climate of violence—and to prove the point many types of so-called violence, from student-protest and ghetto-protest demonstrations to civil disobedience, civil disorders, muggings, and mass murders, are being treated as similar. But demonstrations and civil disobedience are nonviolent, and the civil disorders—ghetto rebellions in actuality—have, with some exceptions, indulged in violence only against property and exploitation. Also, it must not be forgotten that the leaders of S.N.C.C. have not killed anyone, even if their rhetoric has counseled political violence. Indeed, violence against persons has come almost entirely from the protectors of the status quo, and while some of the victims in the ghetto rebellions were killed by panicky members of the police force and the National Guard, others were assassinated by protectors of law and order who were angry that the ghetto wanted social change. Moreover, one cannot compare the political assassinations with the mass murders perpetrated by psychotic individuals such as Speck and Whitman; these killing were in no way politically inspired.

I frankly do not know if American society is sick; we have not yet developed social indicators that measure the health of an entire nation—although we ought to do so. Still, one cannot indict 200 million people for the political murders of three or four noted figures, and it is wrong to describe America as a sick society now if it was not so described when lesser-known men died at the hand of racists and lynchers.

Yet in America there is an excessive amount of homicide, political and nonpolitical, and of nonlethal violence as well, and considerably more than in other Western societies. Much of this violence takes place among the white and black underclasses, however, and I doubt whether there is more violence (or serious mental illness) among affluent Americans than among affluent Englishmen, Swedes, or Russians. The causes of the inordinate amount of American violence, then, are probably to be found in poverty and segregation, for today as in the past, in America and elsewhere, most of society's violence is exerted on the poor or by the poor against each other.

This statistical fact does not exonerate affluent America, though, for America remains responsible for the deprivations that bring on violence among the poor. Whether one is justified in calling America sick depends partly on one's politics. Darwinians might be pleased that it is usually inferiors in the struggle for survival who are being killed off; political conservatives can use the association between violence and poverty to insist that the poor remain undeserving of equality. I would argue that America is opting for an unhealthy amount of social inequality, which presently hurts mainly the unequal, but may soon hurt also those who benefit from our inequality and lack of effective democracy.

Another explanation for the wave of political killings is the presence of sick, demented men in our midst. Undoubtedly such men can be found in all societies, pre-industrial and post-industrial, yet only in America do they seem to become political assassins. Still, it is not at all certain that the assassins were sick. I suspect that most were political killers, hired or self-appointed, who objected to the process of social change sweeping the country.

Yet these killers were not alone, or else they might have been unable to kill. They did—and do—receive encouragement from American culture, which has condoned and even praised political violence while also condemning it. American history is replete with instances of political violence; it began with the killing of the Indians, continued with the draft riots and race riots and the Southern lynchings of the 19th and 20th centuries, and goes on today with the occasional killings by the Ku Klux Klan.

The sad fact is that, like all nations, we sometimes permit the killing of people who do not share our political aims. The most prominent example today is, of course, the war in Vietnam, which we are fighting, among other reasons, in order to kill the Vietcong and the North Vietnamese for believing in a kind of freedom different from our own. Despite the current opposition to this war among many Americans, the political killing by our servicemen is still praised by daily announcements of body counts and is still rewarded by the medals and other honors.

Some now put the blame for the political violence on America's popular culture, particularly on TV and its plethora of fictional murders. TV adventure stories offer a seemingly reasonable explanation for the prevalence of violence in our society, but they also make a convenient scapegoat for people who do not want to define that violence as political (and the Vietnam war as a prime example of such violence), or who want to deny the existence of deprivation and inequality in American life as a cause of political violence.

I do not believe that fictional violence plays a major causal role either in political or nonpolitical violence; American popular culture has always been violent, even before the advent of TV, and other nations have equally violent popular cultures without resorting to political murder. Fictional violence is, after all, fictional; even children know it is unreal and not to be feared. Of course, some TV programs, movies, magazine stories, novels, and comic books allow heroes to kill villains who march to different ideological drummers, and for this reason the popular culture may contribute to the condoning of political murder. Still, it is not a necessary or sufficient cause of such murder.

The news media may, however, play an important if unintentional role in precipitating political assassinations. These media deal in personalities; instead of reporting the social processes and conflicts that create the events we call news, they emphasize principally the leaders, symbolic and real, who participate in these processes. This practice exists for a viable and quite nonpolitical reason: Personalities make far more interesting reading and viewing than sociological analyses. But this practice puts across the idea that events are created by powerful leaders, and exaggerates their actual power in the social processes and conflicts.

The news media build up individuals as all-powerful leaders, thus creating somewhat the same cult of personality for which we criticized the Russians, as David Riesman has pointed out. As a result, potential assassins may think that if they can kill a Martin Luther King or a Robert Kennedy, they can hold back social change. This helps to explain why R.F.K. was killed and Eugene McCarthy not; Robert Kennedy has been "news" for a long time, and his persona and power have been built up and exaggerated. Moreover, power was central to Kennedy's persona; the image of Eugene McCarthy that comes across from the media is of a thoughtful and moral person, but not a powerful leader.

It must be emphasized that the news media did not invent these images and personas; they were only highlighting real phenomena. R.F.K. was and wanted to be powerful; he courted the media treatment he received. More important, the media reflect our culture, which believes that personalities, not social structures, determine events. Ultimately, then, one cannot blame the news media either; they are only part of a more general set of conditions that encourages, or at least condones, political violence. These conditions in turn create a climate in which demented or fanatic individuals can think seriously about turning to political assassination to hold back social change. We may not approve of this climate, but the fact remains that we have not yet acted to create a more peaceful climate for resolving political conflict.

This climate and the social conditions creating it must be changed if the political killing is to stop. But I do not think the killing will stop. Indeed, it may increase as social change accelerates and the country moves toward more equality and democracy. Additional martyrs may be created in the future because those who oppose social change will become more desperate, and will seek to kill leaders whom they identify as responsible for the change.

Nor is it likely that the current call for gun controls will do much to halt political murders. A strict gun law cannot hurt, and if the government could prohibit the further manufacture of guns, and offered to buy up all firearms now in private hands, and put an exorbitant sales tax on bullets, homicide by shooting would decrease, and the danger of racially-inspired black or white vigilante killings might be reduced.

Even so, the most effective way of dealing with political assassination is to accept the reality of social change, to make a determined movement toward equality and democracy in America, and to halt America's intervention in civil wars overseas. If the country's voters and the officials they elect could be made to realize that the demand for equality and democracy cannot be halted, either in this country, in Vietnam, or in the Vietnams of the future, the nation could make a commitment to more effective and less violent forms of change, and the government could then implement policies that would bring about the needed change. If the government is firmly committed to equalization and democratization, if it gives maximal aid to those who now lack these rights and—equally important—to those who will suffer from a change in the status quo, then the nation can begin to accept the inevitability of change, and the resulting social and political climate will probably discourage further political killing.

America has no choice but to create such a climate, because the processes of social change now in motion will not stop. The revolution of rising expectations is in full swing here, perhaps more than in the developing nations. The belief that all men are entitled to control their own lives and to enjoy an equal and democratic share in their society is held not just by poor blacks and by radical college-students, but also by affluent and seemingly conservative people who suffer from inequality and autocracy in their work places and communities. This belief is now too widespread and too intense to be given up, whatever our political leaders do to maintain order. Until this is realized by all of us, however, America may make martyrs out of too many more of its good men, ordinary citizens and leaders alike. And R.F.K., like King, was one of the very best.

July/August 1968

Scapegoats, Villains, and Disasters

THOMAS E. DRABECK/ENRICO L. QUARANTELLI

Disasters, such as the Montgomery, Alabama fire which killed 26 people in February, often bring out the best in individuals. Ability to endure suffering, desire to help others, and acts of courage and generosity come forth in time of crisis. But disasters can also evoke the worst in persons—a relentless search for scapegoats to blame for destruction and loss of life.

This tendency to seek the cause in a *who*—rather than a *what*—is common after airplane crashes, fires, cave-ins, and other catastrophes not caused naturally. Personalizing blame in this way is not only a standard response, but well in harmony with the moral framework of American society. Sin and crime are, after all, matters of personal guilt, by traditional Western legal and theological definitions.

However, social scientists differ in their explanations of what accounts for this personalizing of blame. This can be shown by consideration of three major disasters—the famed

161

Cocoanut Grove night club fire in Boston which killed 498 persons in 1942; the strange sequence of three airplane crashes within three months at Elizabeth, New Jersey, in 1951-52; and the explosion which killed 81 persons in 1963 at the State Fairgrounds Coliseum in Indianapolis.

Social research on disasters has advanced two explanations for this personalizing of blame:

■ It is basically *irrational,* a form of "scapegoating" in which people can work off their frustrations and anxieties, as well as the feelings of guilt, anger, shock, and horror brought on by the disaster.

■ It is relatively *rational,* animated by a desire for prevention of future occurrences. Thus, personalization will take place only when it seems to be within human power to minimize or avoid such disasters, and when it is felt that punishing "the agents of responsibility" may bring forth the necessary remedial action.

The first approach is fully exemplified in a study conducted after the Cocoanut Grove fire. The second is generally illustrated by an analysis of the reactions to the plane crashes into Elizabeth, New Jersey. Following a brief exposition of these two viewpoints, we will suggest a possible new approach to the assessment of blame by considering a more recent disaster—the 1963 explosion in Indianapolis.

The scapegoating process is explicitly expounded by Helen Rank Veltford and George E. Lee in their study of the public reactions to the Cocoanut Grove tragedy. *(The Journal of Abnormal and Social Psychology,* April, 1943) The fire on November 28, 1942, was minor, being extinguished in less than 20 minutes. However, patrons trying to get out found two emergency doors unusable. Also, the major exit, a revolving door, was soon jammed with people. Many of the nearly 500 killed were trapped inside the club and died not only of burns but also of suffocation.

The reaction to this catastrophe was immediate and sharp. According to Veltford and Lee, the horror of the event gave rise to an outcry for avenging the victims and finding and punishing those responsible. Thus, there began a search not primarily for *what* had caused the tragedy, but simply *who* was responsible for it.

Veltford and Lee believe that the public fixing of blame primarily reflected an unconscious effort to relieve blocked emotional reactions or frustrations about what had occurred. There was no immediate public attack on Boston's lax and insufficient laws. Instead, members of the City Council and public officials were blamed for failure to pass more stringent legislation or to enforce existing statutes. After a month of investigation, the county grand jury indicted 10 men.

This personalization is viewed by Veltford and Lee as essential to scapegoating:

The immediate and desired objective of the scapegoaters was to relieve their feelings of frustration, of fear, of hostility, of guilt, by legally fixing the responsibility on the guilty so that they might be punished.

Hence, the attempt to relieve unconscious guilt feelings resulted in irrational behavior; the selection of a series of scapegoats rather than demand for stricter and better laws.

However, the researchers point out that certain logical candidates were not chosen as scapegoats. For example, no blame was attached to the 16-year-old employee who actually started the fire by striking a match for light while replacing a missing bulb. Why not? According to Veltford and Lee it was because the public admired his straightforward voluntary admission of fault, because of his youth, and the fact that his mother was seriously ill. His teachers testified he was a model young man from an impoverished family. Of such things scapegoats are not made. The prankster who had presumably removed the bulb was not blamed either, because nobody knew who he was and because he was certainly not the direct cause of the fire, much less the deaths.

Those seeking someone to blame had "more satisfying" scapegoats to relieve their guilt feelings. Ten prominent persons and officials, including the owners of the club and the Boston Building Commissioner, were indicted and charged with a variety of offenses: conspiracy to violate building codes, failure to enforce fire laws, failure to report violations of the building laws, and so forth. Collectively they were "the rascals, for among certain elements of the public there is a deep-rooted, perhaps unrecognized latent hostility toward all political authority, toward those 'higher up.' " All accumulated past hostilities against "political bigwigs" and "money czars" could be focused on the two classes of scapegoats, owners and public officials: ". . . Elements of the public may have found opportunity to *enhance* their own self-conceived prestige; they could, by scapegoating, feel, momentarily, superior to these so-called 'higher ups.' "

Finally, as Martha Wolfenstein has documented in a review of the disaster literature, people find it difficult to blame the dead. It was the panic of the Cocoanut Grove victims that led to the blocked exit and a fatal crush—but no one blamed them for it. Wolfenstein found, in fact, that in a 1955 French race track disaster, a driver who crashed into the spectators was viewed as a savior rather than an "agent of destruction" because he saved the lives of other drivers by avoiding collisions. She concludes that an individual who survives disaster feels guilty for not having died himself. "Probably the more latent hostility there is present in an individual the greater will be his need to blame either himself or others for destructive happenings."

From this first perspective then, attribution of blame following disaster is typical and is motivated by unconscious guilt and related feelings. Such motivations produce a variety of irrational behaviors among which scapegoating is common. "Innocent" persons are selected on the basis of latent hostilities from a guilt-ridden populace.

In sharp contrast is the position advanced by Rue Bucher. *(American Journal of Sociology,* March, 1957) She analyzed reactions of residents of Elizabeth, New Jersey, in 1951-52 to three airplane crashes within a three-month period. Rather than being a *common feature* of disasters, Bucher suggests that individuals will be blamed only when *certain specific* conditions are present:

■ The situation must be defined sufficiently to assess responsibility. This occurs only when conventional explanations are not available. For example, in present day Western society, probably no person will be assigned direct responsibility for destruction caused by tornadoes, floods, and hurricanes. Damage and deaths from such events can be conventionally accounted for in non-personal and naturalistic terms.

■ ". . . Those who blame the agents of responsibility are convinced that the agents will not of their own volition take action which will remedy the situation."

■ ". . . Those responsible must be perceived as violating moral standards, as standing in opposition to basic values."

Bucher believes the primary motive is a desire to insure that it does not happen again. As a consequence, the attribution of responsibility tends to be shifted upward in the hierarchy of authority. Persons who may have had a direct hand in the catastrophe, such as the airline pilots, are not blamed. Bucher says that responsibility is ". . . laid where people thought the power resided to alleviate the conditions underlying the crashes. It was not instrumentality in causing the crashes which determined responsibility but ability to do something to prevent their recurrence. The problem was who had control over these conditions and who had the power to see that they were corrected."

In Elizabeth, specific blame was not placed—only a generalized "they" was held responsible for failure to take action. Bucher attributes this to the limited knowledge her lower and middle class respondents had about airlines, airports, and the industries and agencies that affect them.

From this perspective then, assessment of responsibility and personal blame has at least some subjective rationality. The chief desire is to prevent recurrence. Only when natural explanations are not enough will persons be blamed. If it is felt that appropriate action will not be taken by the "agents of responsibility," then blame will be assigned to those believed to have the power to change existing conditions. There are no buckshot accusations; specific names and charges depend on knowledge of persons and groups.

Actually, differences between the two viewpoints described above are primarily differences of interpretation of human behavior after disasters. There is a close parallel in the gross descriptions of that behavior. However, a study made by the authors of this article after the Indianapolis Coliseum explosion indicates the possibilities of a third explanation—one that places blame assessment into a much broader framework.

At 11:06 p.m., on October 31, 1963, a performance of the "Holiday on Ice" show at the Indianapolis Coliseum was abruptly ended by a violent blast. Fifty-four persons were killed immediately, nearly 400 were injured. Twenty-seven of the injured died later, raising the final death count to 81, the largest toll in any Indiana disaster.

Press, radio, and television personnel went into action immediately. Initial coverage was on the rescue operations, identification of victims, and descriptions. But attention quickly focused on the cause and the responsibility. When liquid propane gas tanks found in the rubble were suspected of causing the explosion, the media quickly pressed forward on this trail.

Interest intensified throughout the night. The three major newspapers carried these headlines on their first editions after the disaster: "FIRE CHIEF RAPS GAS TANK USAGE IN THE COLISEUM"; "PROBE PRESSED BY BLAST THAT KILLED HERE"; "65 KILLED, HUNDREDS HURT IN COLISEUM GAS EXPLOSION." On November 1 the Marion County prosecutor requested the grand jury to begin an immediate investigation.

The spotlight was kept relentlessly focused on possible responsibility. For instance, the evening following the explosion the state fire marshal was pressed to admit in a televised interview that apparently no one had applied for or obtained the necessary permit to use liquid gas inside the Coliseum.

Formal investigations were conducted by at least nine different organizations. They included: the Indianapolis fire department, the Indianapolis police department, the state police, the Marion County sheriff's office, the State Administrative Building Council, the state fire marshal, the county coroner's office, and the company insuring the State Fair Board and the Indiana Coliseum Corporation. Mostly they concentrated on the physical cause of the explosion. This was a response at least in part to inquiries by the mass media trying to fix personal responsibility.

The grand jury completed its investigation in early December after five weeks of inquiry during which repeated trips to the scene of the disaster were made, and thirty-two witnesses were questioned. LP gas, illegally stored inside the Coliseum, was judged to have caused the explosion. Seven persons were indicted—three officials of the firm supplying the tanks, the general manager and the concession manager of the Indiana Coliseum Corporation, the state fire marshal, and the Indianapolis fire chief.

These events can effectively be interpreted within the framework suggested by Bucher. The illegal presence of the five LP gas tanks, and the quick identification by the media of the public and private officials who had been involved in their installation lent plausibility to a personal and non-naturalistic explanation of the explosion.

There were two additional elements. First, newspaper accounts suggested that previous warnings had not brought action. For instance, *The Indianapolis Star* reported that a check of official records indicated the fire marshal's office had been warned of leaking propane gas in the Coliseum on September 3, 1959. They stopped its use that day, but the next day inspectors were again notified of leaking LP gas at the Coliseum. This resulted in a declaration by the chief inspector from the fire marshal's office that he did not have an adequate staff to enforce fire regulations properly. Representatives from the Coliseum countered that LP gas tanks had been openly used for 10 years, but no one had ever told them they needed a permit. Hence, it was implied that the "agents of responsibility" could not be trusted to correct conditions.

It was even indicated that criticism by the grand jury would not bring about any change. The governor openly defended his fire marshal. He alleged that the grand jury had used public officials as "scapegoats," and added that the fire marshal had generally done a good job and would remain in office.

Of course, from a sociological viewpoint the issue is not whether the charges were true, but whether—and to what extent—they were made public and how people viewed them. It is, after all, an old axiom in sociology that "if a situation is defined as real, it is real insofar as consequences are concerned." Press reports clearly implied that some of those in power might not make changes necessary to prevent similar accidents in the future.

Further, words used in the indictments implied that the "agents of responsibility" were socially irresponsible if not immoral. The grand jury felt that some control over future uses of LP gas was needed to ". . . guarantee that the desire for profit on the part of a few will never again relegate the matter of public safety to a point of reckless indifference." The report further stated that "the fire marshal was considered (political) patronage, and he acted the part."

Thus, all of the elements suggested by Bucher as being necessary for blame were present.

Also, blame was focused high in the authority structures. Indictments were directed at the fire chief, not the city fire inspectors; the state fire marshal, not his agents; top executives of the firm supplying the tanks, not the individuals who actually installed them; and the executives of the Coliseum Corporation, not the concessionaires who used the tanks.

Thus, the facts seem to fit the Bucher interpretation. But could not these same facts be made to support the scapegoating theory? Those indicted for the Cocoanut Grove fire were also of high status. Could not those indicted as a result of the Coliseum explosion have really been selected because of irrational latent hostilities against "big shots"?

Closer reading of the grand jury report, however, renders such an interpretation improbable. Consistently there is reference to the need for changes in existing law, including on-site and possibly stand-by inspection during actual performances. The jury also labeled the permit system "archaic and useless," and wanted the entire state fire marshal's office reorganized "from top to bottom." Finally, it urged legislation to make violation of regulations by the fire marshal a crime.

Thus the prime interest of the grand jury was apparently for changes in organizations and laws to prevent similar disasters.

But in that case why did it not take specific steps to bring about such changes? Why did it merely indict persons? As we see it, personal blame assignment in American society cannot be avoided; it is rooted in the institutional framework. Investigative agencies are bound by laws that force them "to point the finger" only at persons who are potentially legally prosecutable. The grand jury might think the system to blame; but under the law it could only bring legal charges against human beings. Only individuals can be indicted and brought to trial—not social structures.

This was the situation at Indianapolis. There was some awareness that the problem touched the very roots of the system; but its solution was approached in the usual and almost necessary way. Only the traditional legal processes (i.e., a grand jury, indictments, trials and so forth) were utilized. The machinery for coping with these situations was not geared toward changing the social structure. The political-legal processes could only condemn individuals and ask for their punishment. The verbal assault in the mass media probably also served as another pressure on the grand jury to indict persons—and thereby weaken the call for other action.

The rationale is that punishment of the "guilty" deters others from committing similar acts. However, many sociologists suggest that this whole orientation with its focus on personal "guilt" and "innocence" may actually serve to delay necessary changes by concentrating on symptoms rather than causes. Paul B. Horton and Gerald R. Leslie note, for instance, that: "To many people, 'doing something' about a social problem means finding and punishing the 'bad' people." The consequence is that "punishing the 'bad' people, . . . will have very little permanent effect upon the problem." It may act to hinder its solution.

The way blame was fixed in Indianapolis illustrates this. A basic structural element—the inspection procedure— was obviously indequate. Only 12 investigators were expected to provide inspection for the entire state of Indiana. One had to cover 4,000 square miles. They only had power to issue impotent "cease and desist" orders. Both the fire marshal and the state inspectors were political appointees; no objective selection procedures existed for either position. Yet by blaming individuals, attention was taken away from all of this.

We believe that putting other persons into the same position could have made little difference. The fire marshal's staff, for instance, was so indequate both in quantity and quality that meaningful preventive action by any fire marshal was impossible. Similarly, economic factors were alleged to have been responsible for inadequate safety training for the employees who installed or used the LP tanks.

In essence we are saying that the entire procedure used to remedy the conditions that caused the disaster may well be questioned. As Robert K. Merton and Robert A. Nesbit have pointed out, social problems may not always be recognized as such by those most intimately involved. Sociologists cannot restrict themselves to those social conditions that a majority of laymen regard as undesirable. The majority is not always knowledgeable enough to be a good judge of what is undesirable. Not all "processes of society inimical to the values of men are recognized as such by them."

Not only does individual blame draw attention from

more fundamental causes, but it might actually give the illusion that corrective action of some sort is being taken. A spotlighting by the mass media may give the appearance of action and actually drain off the energy and time that might have led to action. As Merton and Paul F. Lazarsfeld have noted, greater information and publicity can actually create civic apathy. Public attention focused on punishment does not encourage action to correct structural flaws. In the example of the Indianapolis Coliseum, the inadequate inspection procedure remained submerged, hidden by the search for the guilty parties.

It is of more than passing interest that in another major disaster studied by the Disaster Research Center the absence of personal blame was accompanied by relatively rapid and major structural changes. On November 23, 1963, a nursing home fire in Ohio resulted in the death of 63 patients. Several investigations revealed many of the same, if not even greater, general weaknesses in the fire inspection procedures found in Indiana. However, there was little time spent looking for people to "blame" for the tragedy. A Grand Jury failed to indict anyone; no persons or officials were held responsible; and everyone connected with the event was exonerated. Yet within a few months, major and stringent new rules and regulations were put into effect throughout the state. Nursing homes not meeting the new standards were forced to close. Had this event not occurred, it is doubtful that new standards would have been enacted.

By contrast, in Indiana, more than three years after the disaster, not even personal blame had been settled. In early 1967 all legal cases were still pending except those against the owner and the general manager of the firm that supplied the tanks. The former had been found not guilty; the charge against the latter had been reduced from involuntary manslaughter to assault and battery, and he had been fined $500. The charge against the Indianapolis fire chief had been dismissed quite early. The other four persons charged still remained under indictment.

As for any structural changes, even less had occurred. Some of the procedures—nothing substantial—had been altered in the fire marshal's office. In 1966, a seven-man bipartisan Fire Prevention Commission with supervisory power over the office had been established, but no major internal reorganization had occurred. For a time, fewer people attended events at the reopened Coliseum; but within a year, capacity and standing room audiences were back for some shows. Except for those most directly involved, the community had returned to its pre-disaster patterns.

It would be foolish to argue that personal blame assignment always prevents structural changes. There is indeed historical evidence to suggest that some disastrous events have an impact. For example, the first international code of maritime safety laws came in 1914, two years after the sinking of the *Titanic;* the latest in 1960, four years after the loss of the *Andrea Doria.* In the famous Triangle Shirtwaist factory fire in New York City (March 28, 1911), 145 workers were killed, and the owners were indicted for manslaughter; and yet within months new laws were passed, giving fire inspectors increased powers, establishing a division of fire prevention, and forcing changes in rules regarding fire prevention, drills, alarm systems, sprinklers, and fire escapes.

Even in Boston, three years after the Cocoanut Grove fire it could be written: "Under the impetus given by the worst fire in the city's history, the state is on its way to a system of building and inspecting regulations that may become a model." How much real change resulted and how much the basic structural flaws were affected, are of course matters that would have to be more fully studied.

Yet these examples certainly suggest that punishment of "guilty individuals" *per se* does not automatically prevent some structural changes.

Personalizing fault—blaming our problems on the inadequacies or guilt of individuals rather than on systems or institutions—is not confined to disasters. Something akin to it has been observed in every aspect of American life from the content of movies dealing with social problems to the assumptions being made in the present day "war on poverty." Thus Herbert Gans has noted of certain kinds of contemporary films:

> Psychological explanations have replaced moral ones, but the possibility that delinquency, corruption and even mental illness reside in the social system is not considered, and the resolution of the problem is still left to a hero assisted by the everpresent *deus ex machina.*

S. A. Weinstock, on the approach to poverty problems:

> The underlying assumption here again is that poverty, social and economic deprivation, results from an inadequacy of the personality rather than an inadequacy in the socio-economic system. . . . Only measures aiming at individual rehabilitation . . . are encouraged, while measures designed to modify the *structure* of the economy . . . are rejected.

On race riots, Stanley Liberson and Arnold Silverman:

> Accounts . . . attributing riots to communist influence, hoodlums, or rabblerousers . . . participants of this type are probably available in almost any community. What interests us is the community failure to see the . . . institutional malfunctioning or a racial difficulty which is not—and perhaps cannot—be met by existing social institutions.

As with blame after disasters, here too the fault-finding seems rooted in the very fabric of American society. Here also it distracts attention from structural flaws. If the individual is the source of all difficulties, why raise questions about the society?

Apparently it is not only in totalitarian societies that a "cult of personality" serves to protect existing structures, and keeps them from making rapid changes to meet important cultural values and goals—even if those changes might be vital to the welfare of the society.

March 1967

FURTHER READINGS SUGGESTED BY THE AUTHORS:

Social Organization Under Stress: A Sociological Review of Disaster Studies, Allen Barton (Washington: National Academy of Sciences, 1963). Excellent presentation of a sociological perspective on disaster behavior.

Contemporary Social Problems, Robert K. Merton and Robert A. Nisbet eds. (New York: Harcourt, Brace and World, 1961). Good discussion of social problems and best overall summary of disaster responses, in chapter by Charles E. Fritz.

Disaster, Disaster, Disaster: Catastrophes Which Changed Laws, Douglas Newton ed. (New York: Franklin Watts, 1961). Non-scholarly but provocative examination of disaster aftermaths.

What
Looting in Civil Disturbances
Really Means

RUSSELL DYNES/ENRICO L. QUARANTELLI

In March and April of this year, there were civil disturbances in Memphis, Tenn., Washington, D.C.,
Chicago, Pittsburgh, and Baltimore. Many films and
photographs were taken of people looting other
people's property. These looting incidents conformed
to the pattern, for according to many reports people
may be found looting when a community is having
certain kinds of crises. One of these crises is caused
by a natural disaster—a flood, hurricane, and so forth.
And the other is caused by a civil disturbance, like
the ones that have hit American cities every summer
since the Watts outbreak of August 1965.

Natural disasters and civil disturbances give people
a chance to help themselves to other people's goods.
Yet there are important, fascinating differences between what happens in these two crisis situations.
For example, looting is far more common in civil

disturbances than in disasters. Then too, the *kinds* of goods taken during these two crises are different. And public disdain for the act varies. Sometimes taking other people's property during a community crisis is not even considered looting!

In order to examine the differences between the two crisis situations, let us analyze what happens to private property during natural disasters, and then contrast this with the transfers of property that take place during civil disorders.

The word "looting" has military roots. It implies that invading armies take property by force, generally when the rightful owner cannot protect it. Similarly, in civil disturbances "invading armies" plunder property left unguarded when the owner is forced out by violence or the threat of violence. During disasters, according to common belief, "invading armies" of opportunists take property left unguarded when the owner is forced out by the disaster.

The looting that takes place in these situations is usually interpreted as evidence of human depravity. In periods of natural or civil chaos, goes the explanation, the human animal is stripped of his usual social controls. Without them, he is not a noble savage, but an ignoble one. For the general public, reports of looting are easy to incorporate into their images of the "criminal elements" who clean out the corner grocery during a racial disturbance, or the fiends and ghouls who roam disaster-stricken areas.

After the Galveston hurricane of 1900, published accounts told of people being summarily shot when they were caught with pocketsful of severed fingers with rings on them. In 1906, after the San Francisco earthquake and fire, the *Los Angeles Times* reported that "looting by fiends incarnate made a hell broth of the center of the ruined district. Sixteen looters were shot out of hand on April 19, while robbing the dead." In his reconstruction of events after the earthquake, reporter Q.A. Bronson noted "reports . . . of . . . looters wantonly shot in their tracks by Federal troops, miscreants hanged in public squares, and ghouls found cutting off the fingers and ears of corpses for rings and earrings attached."

Today, most radio and television accounts of disasters are less dramatic, but looting is still a major theme. After a tornado hit some suburbs of Chicago in April 1967, a county sheriff reportedly announced that "orders had gone out that beginning at 10 P.M. Friday, any looters . . . were to be shot on sight." After a power failure blacked out the Cincinnati area in May 1967, a wire-service story told of the smashing of store windows and looting in Cincinnati and in neighboring Newport and Covington, Ky.

Public officials, expecting certain kinds of community emergencies to activate human depravity, often request additional law enforcement. They mobilize National Guard units and take extra security measures. These steps are often taken upon the first reports of a civil disturbance or a natural disaster. Frequently, before the situation has even developed, television and radio will report what *is expected to happen*—the fear of looting and the steps being taken to prevent it.

That most people are concerned about looting in civil disorders and disasters is beyond dispute. Reliable evidence, however, points to a surprising fact: While looting clearly does occur in civil disturbances, in disaster situations it is very rare.

Many studies of disasters mention *reports* of looting,

but very few cite authenticated cases. One study that did inquire into actual cases of looting was the National Opinion Research Center (N.O.R.C.) study of White County, Ark., after it was ravaged by a tornado in 1952. In the community that suffered the greatest damage, about 1000 of the 1200 residents were left homeless. A random sample of people from this town and adjacent areas were asked whether they had lost any property by looting. Only 9 percent reported that they, or members of their immediate household, had lost property that they even *felt* had been taken by looters. And fully one-third of these people were uncertain whether the loss was really due to looters, or whether the missing items had been blown away or buried in the debris. Finally, most of the articles were of little value.

In contrast, 58 percent of the people questioned said they had heard of *others'* property being stolen. In fact, 9 percent claimed that they had even seen looting in progress or had seen looters being arrested. The N.O.R.C. study team on the scene, however, could verify the theft of only two major items—a cash register and a piano.

Other disaster research confirms the rarity of looting. A study made after the 1953 floods in the Netherlands found that, although there were many reports of looting, law-enforcement agencies could discover not a single verified case. The Dutch researchers attributed many of the reports of looting to memory lapses in the immediate post-flood period, and pointed out that a number of people who reported thefts later found the missing items. Charles Fritz and J.H. Mathewson, in a review of disaster studies published up to 1956, concluded that "the number of verified cases of actual looting in peacetime disasters, in the United States and in foreign countries, is small."

More recent studies point in the same direction. The Disaster Research Center at Ohio State University, in field studies of more than 40 disasters both in the United States and abroad, has found extremely few verified cases of looting. Actual police records support these findings. For example, in September 1965, the month Hurricane Betsy struck New Orleans, major crimes in the city fell 26.6 percent below the rate for the same month in the previous year. Burglaries reported to the police fell from 617 to 425. Thefts of over $50 dropped from 303 to 264, and those under $50 fell from 516 to 366.

Since all evidence is that looting is rare or non-existent in natural disasters, why do reports of looting in disaster situations occur over and over again? And why are these reports persistently believed, even when there is no clear evidence to back them up?

To answer these questions, we need to look at four conditions that usually prevail in the immediate post-impact period: misinterpretations of observed behavior; misunderstandings over property ownership; inflated reports of looting; and sensational coverage of disaster situations by the news media.

Reports of looting are often based on misinterpretation of people's motives. After a disaster, masses of people—often numbering in the thousands—converge on the impact area. Local officials, particularly those with little experience in large-scale emergencies, frequently regard these convergers as sightseers—and, by extension, as potential looters. However, Fritz and Mathewson have shown that there are at least five different types of convergers: the returnees—the disaster survivors who want to go back to the impact area; the anxious—those concerned with the safety of kin and friends; the helpers—those who want to donate their services; the curious—those attempting to make some sense out of the unusual events that have occurred; and the exploiters—those seeking private gain from public misfortune. The number in this last category is small and includes, in addition to potential looters, souvenir hunters, relief stealers, and profiteers.

The important point is that those who converge on a disaster area have a variety of motives. Community officials often do not seem to recognize this. For example, a property owner whose house has been destroyed may return to the area to sift through the debris of his own home in the hope of recovering lost articles. To a casual observer, his behavior may look like looting. Out-of-town relatives may come into a disaster area with a truck to help their kin collect and store their remaining possessions. People engaged in informal search-and-rescue activities of this sort may also appear to be looters. The souvenir hunter is looking for something that has symbolic rather than material value. But in the disaster context, his behavior too becomes suspect.

Another source of false looting reports is the fact that, although little or no property is stolen in disaster situations, goods are frequently given away. Sometimes there is confusion about which items are free, and who is entitled to them.

In one disaster, the report began circulating that a grocery store had been looted. Investigation revealed that the owner had placed damaged goods outside on the sidewalk, announcing that anyone was welcome to take them. Since his store front had been demolished, however, the line between the free goods and the owner's undamaged stock was vague—and some people who came to get the free goods inadvertently took items from the undamaged stock instead. This misunderstanding was soon cleared up. But an early report of the incident, given to the military authorities in the area, quickly spread throughout the community as an authentic case of looting. And what's more, the looting report was later accepted as valid even by members of the military who had established that it was false.

Overblown estimates of disaster losses are the third source of unfounded looting reports. Officials in a disaster area frequently tend to overestimate the seriousness of the situation. Messages about either the quantity of aid needed or the extent of the damage tend to mushroom as they pass from one person to another. If one official asks another for 100 cots, the second official may relay a request to a third official for 150 cots, and so on. In much the same way, reports of looting get blown out of proportion.

The following incident occurred at a communications center in a major metropolitan area that had been hit by a hurricane: A patrolman in the field, talking over his radio, made a casual comment that, since some store fronts were open and could easily be entered, perhaps a policeman might be dispatched to that location. The patrolman who received this call was busy for a few minutes with other queries. Then he made a call to the state police requesting that a force be rushed to that location—since, he said, "a hell of a lot of looting is going on there."

Sensational news accounts round out the picture. Naturally, the mass media emphasize the dramatic. The atypical and the unique are what catch the newsman's attention. Photographs of disaster areas depict the buildings that are destroyed, not the ones that are still intact. And in press accounts, any stories about looting—including the stories that are inaccurate and inflated—are quickly seized upon and highlighted.

These accounts are often accepted as reasonable descriptions of what is occurring even by community officials themselves. In the absence of up-to-date and direct information, what happened or what is happening is not easy to determine. The phone system may be disrupted, preventing direct feedback of information from field points. Movement may be severely restricted. Direct observation is often impossible. And the pressure for immediate action may prevent anyone from keeping accurate records. Since few people in any community have much first-hand experience with large-scale disasters, journalistic accounts become a major means of defining reality. As one police chief said in reply to a question about his knowledge of looting, "Well, I'm not sure. All I know right now is the reports I've heard over the radio."

The upshot of all this is that many reported cases of post-disaster "looting," based on misinterpretation or misunderstanding and publicized by exaggerated or sensational accounts, are not really cases of looting at all. They involve no unlawful appropriations of property.

Still, the fact remains that certain "illegal" appropriations of property *do* occur in disaster situations. For example, people sometimes break into stores and warehouses without the owner's consent and take medical supplies, cots, generators, and flashlights. Now, is this looting? And if not, why not?

Here we come to the critical element of "property

redefinition." Incidents of this sort are *not* looting. The notion of "property" involves a shared understanding about who can do what with the valued resources within a community. When a disaster strikes, property rights are temporarily redefined: There is general agreement among community members that the resources of individuals become *community property*. Individual property rights are suspended, so appropriation of private resources—which would normally be considered looting—is temporarily condoned. Before these resources can be given back to private use, the needs of the disoriented larger community have to be met.

When a natural crisis occurs, the usual plurality of individual goals gives way to the single, overriding goal of the community—the goal of saving as many lives as possible. Any way of achieving this becomes legitimate. People who are trapped have to be rescued; people who are in dangerous areas have to be evacuated; people who have been injured have to be given medical attention; people who are missing, and perhaps injured, must be found. If this means community appropriation of private search equipment, medical material, and even vehicles, it is implicitly viewed as necessary. In one case, a city attorney even made it official: He announced that people were to disregard any laws that would interfere with the search-and-rescue efforts going forward in the central part of the city. This meant formally sanctioning breaking into and entering private stores and offices in the city.

The redefinition of property that occurs during natural disasters, then, almost defines looting out of existence. Almost, but not quite. For implicit in the redefinition is the idea that access to the redefined property is limited to community members, and for community ends. If outsiders enter the disaster area and begin appropriating private property for their own use, it is still looting. And in fact, evidence indicates that the few verified instances of looting that do occur in natural disasters are almost always of this sort— that is, they are committed by outsiders.

Occasionally there are authenticated reports that seem to contradict our finding that looting in natural disasters is very rare. One example is the looting that occurred during the very heavy snowstorms that paralyzed Chicago in late January and early February 1967. A few of the incidents reported were probably routine burglaries, but others were clearly looting. They were not randomly distributed by location, and most of the cases occurred in the same neighborhoods—and sometimes on exactly the same streets—where looting had taken place in the civil disturbances during the summer months of 1966. Along Chicago's Roosevelt Road, for example, looting took place on some of the very same blocks.

This suggests that the looting that occurred in Chicago during the snowstorm was actually a continuation, or perhaps a resurgence, of the earlier civil disturbance. For the general public, the habit of viewing civil disturbances as exclusively summer events probably obscured the true nature of the snowstorm looting. But some local policemen clearly interpreted the looting as a winter recurrence of the summer's civil disorders.

In contrast to what happens in a disaster situation, looting in civil disturbances is widespread, and the looters are usually members of the immediate community. During the past few summers, films and photographs have shown looting actually in progress. The McCone

Commission reported that about 600 stores were looted or burned in Watts. In Newark, around 1300 people were arrested, mostly for taking goods. In the July 1967 holocaust in Detroit, unofficial estimates were that about 2700 stores were ransacked.

Disasters and civil disturbances are alike in that the normal order and organization of the community is disrupted. In addition, there is, in both situations, a temporary redefinition of property rights. But the two situations differ in other respects. In a disaster, there is general agreement among community members about community goals, especially about saving lives. As a result, by general agreement, all the resources are put at the disposal of the total community until emergency needs are met. A civil disturbance, on the other hand, represents conflict—not consensus—on community goals. The outbreak itself represents disagreement over property rights within the community. Access to existing resources is questionable, and often there is open challenge to prior ownership.

The critical role of attitudes toward property in determining the nature of looting is best seen by contrasting the looting that occurs in civil disturbances with that found in disasters. There are three significant differences. As already noted, widespread looting *does* occur in civil disturbances, while it is infrequent in disasters. Further, the looting in civil disturbances is selective, focusing on particular types of goods or possessions, often symbolic of other values. And, while out-and-out looting is strongly condemned in disaster situations, looters in civil disturbances receive, from certain segments of the local community, strong social support for their actions.

The occurrence of looting in civil disturbances needs

no further documentation. And selectivity can be seen in the fact that, in racial outbreaks, looters have concentrated overwhelmingly on certain kinds of stores. In Watts, Newark, and Detroit, the main businesses affected were groceries, supermarkets, and furniture and liquor stores. In contrast, banks, utility stations, industrial plants, and private residences have been generally ignored. Apartments and homes have been damaged, but only because they were in or near burned business establishments. Public installations such as schools and Office of Economic Opportunity centers have also been spared. There has not been indiscriminate looting. Certain kinds of consumer goods have been almost the only targets.

Looters in civil disturbances are also likely to receive support from many people in their community. Spiraling support coincides with shifts in property redefinitions, and these shifts occur in three stages. Initial looting is often a symbolic act of defiance. The second phase, in which more conscious and deliberate plundering develops, is possibly spurred on by the presence of delinquent gangs that loot more from need or for profit than for ideological reasons. Finally, in the third stage, there is widespread seizure of goods. At this point, looting becomes the socially expected thing to do. For example, a sociological survey at U.C.L.A. found that nearly one-fourth of the population participated in the Watts outbreak (although all of these participants probably did not engage in the looting).

If looting means strictly the taking of goods, little of it occurs in the first phase of civil disturbances. Instead, destructive attacks are most frequently directed against symbols of authority in the community. Police cars and fire trucks are pillaged and burned. What is involved here is perhaps illustrated most clearly in other kinds of civil disturbances, such as some of those created by college students. One of the authors once watched a crowd of students determinedly attack, for over an hour, an overhead traffic light. It conveniently symbolized the city administration and police—the actual target of the demonstrators' wrath. In racial civil disturbances, the police and their equipment are also seen as obvious symbols of the larger community toward which the outbreak is directed. How intense this focus can be was shown in the Watts disturbance. About 168 police cars and 100 pieces of fire-fighting equipment were damaged or destroyed.

The full redefinition of certain property rights occurs next. The "carnival spirit" observed in the Newark and Detroit disturbances did not represent anarchy. It represented widespread social support for the new definition of property. In this phase, there is little competition for goods. In fact, in contrast to the stealthy looting that occasionally occurs in disaster situations, looting in civil disturbances is quite open and frequently collective. The looters often work together in pairs, as family units, or in small groups. Bystanders are frequently told about potential loot. And in some instances, as in the Watts outbreak, looters coming out of stores hand strangers goods as "gifts."

Looting in civil disturbances is by insiders—by local community members. These looters apparently come not only from the low socioeconomic levels and from delinquent gangs, but from all segments of the population. During disturbances in Toledo, 91 percent of the 126 adults arrested for taking goods had jobs. A random sample in Detroit found that participants in the outbreak came more or less equally from all income brackets.

In both disasters and civil disturbances, there is a redefinition of property rights within the community. The community authorities, however, respond very differently to the two situations. In disasters, responsible officials tolerate, accept, and encourage the transition from private to community property. In civil disturbances, community authorities see looting as essentially criminal behavior—as a legal problem to be handled forcefully by the police. And many segments of the larger community, especially middle-class people, with their almost sacred conception of private property, tend to hold the same view. This view of looting in civil disturbances fits in neatly with the ideas they already have about the criminal propensities of certain ethnic groups, notably Negroes.

At one level, there is no question that looting in civil disturbances is criminal behavior. But the laws that make it so are themselves based on dominant conceptions of property rights. Widespread looting, then, may perhaps be interpreted as a kind of mass protest against our dominant conceptions of property.

Mass protest is not new in history. According to George Rudé's analysis, in his book *The Crowd in History,* demonstrating mobs from 1730 to 1848 in England and France were typically composed of local, respectable, employed people rather than the pauperized, the unemployed, or the "rabble" of the slums. The privileged classes naturally regarded these popular agitations as criminal—as fundamentally and unconditionally illegitimate. Rudé notes, however, that such protest effectively communicated the desires of a segment of the urban population to the élite. E.J. Hobsbawm, in his analysis of the preindustrial "city mob," takes the same position: "The classical mob did not merely riot as a protest, but because it expected to achieve something by its riot. It assumed that the authorities would be sensitive to its movements, and probably also that they would make some immediate concession. . . . This mechanism was perfectly understood by both sides."

In current civil disturbances, a similar mechanism and a similar message may be evolving. An attack against property rights is not necessarily "irrational," "criminal," or "pointless" if it leads to a clearer system of demands and responses, in which the needs and obligations of the contending parties are reasonably clear to themselves and to one another. The scope and intensity of current attacks indicate the presence of large numbers of outsiders living within most American cities. If property is seen as a shared understanding about the allocation of resources, and if a greater consensus can be reached on the proper allocation of these resources, many of these outsiders will become insiders, with an established stake in the communities in which they live.

This, then, is the most fundamental way in which looting in civil disturbances differs from looting after natural disasters: The looting that has occurred in recent racial outbreaks is a bid for the redistribution of property. It is a message that certain deprived sectors of the population want what they consider their fair share—and that they will resort to violence to get it. The fact that looting in riots is more widespread than in disasters, that it concentrates on the prestige items that symbolize the good life, and that it receives the support and approval of many within the deprived sectors who do not participate themselves, merely indicates the true nature and intention of looting under conditions of mass protest.

The basic question now is whether American community leaders can or will recognize that such looting is more than "pointless" or "criminal" behavior. 'If they do, it may mark the beginning of a new political dialogue, in which the outsiders in our urban communities can express their desires nonviolently to the insiders— insiders who will have finally learned to listen. If not, then in the summers to come, and perhaps in the winters as well, many men and women from the growing urban population may continue to demand a redefinition of property rights through disorder and violence.

May 1968

FURTHER READING SUGGESTED BY THE AUTHORS:

Social Organization Under Stress: A Sociological Review of Disaster Studies by Allen Barton (Washington: National Academy of Sciences, 1963). An excellent summary of research on disaster behavior.

Convergence Behavior in Disasters by Charles Fritz and J.H. Mathewson (Washington, D.C.: National Academy of Sciences, 1957). An excellent analysis of actual social control problems in disasters.

The Impossible Revolution? Black Power and the American Dream by Lewis Killian (New York: Random House, 1968). A projection into the future of current trends in civil disorders.

Riots, Violence and Disorder: Civil Turbulence in Urban Communities edited by Louis Masotti (Beverly Hills, Calif.: Sage Publications, 1968). A series of wide-ranging articles on urban disturbances.